**Dedicated to
Gregory Andre Chevalley
1971–2014**

I know you're smiling in heaven somewhere,
with a half grin, shaking your head at me and
saying 'Finally I taught you something Shelly'.
This book is for you Greg, and all the other
good souls that pass away too early from this
precious, wonderful life. You were one hell of
a fireman and human, and taught me to live –
really live – now, today and abundantly.

EAT
DRINK
& STILL
SHRINK

EAT DRINK & STILL SHRINK

MICHELE
CHEVALLEY HEDGE

Pan Macmillan Australia

Michele is always seeking
evidence-based, high quality
research to underpin her writing.
As recognition of the good work
they do, a percentage of the
proceeds of the sale of this
book will be donated to
The Food & Mood Centre
at Deakin University.

Contents

Introduction

'And the day came when the risk to remain tight in a bud was more painful than the risk it took to blossom.'

ANAIS NIN

I can't remember the exact day, but I remember exactly what happened – and most of all, how I felt. I was getting ready for work. I was on one of my starve-binge-starve cycles, and I felt enormous. I was chubby, about 10 kilos overweight, and bloated. My skirt was too tight. My jacket was uncomfortable on my ever-growing nana arms. Even pulling up my stockings was awkward. But I got dressed anyway, because I had to go to work.

When I went to put my make-up on, I found I couldn't even look in the mirror. If I was uncomfortable in my clothes, it was positively excruciating to look at myself. I was so fed up, distressed, anxious and irritable about the way I looked that I couldn't stand to look at my own reflection. So I didn't.

I went and found a small square mirror and shuffled up to it at an awkward angle, so that when I tilted my head a certain way I could just barely see my eyeball in the corner of the mirror. I couldn't see my body at all. I could see enough to apply my mascara, but not enough to make me feel terrible about myself. What a way to live, huh?

Even if I was able to ignore my growing body and my plummeting self-esteem for a moment, it all came flooding back the minute I stepped away from that mirror. And that was it. That was the day that the risk to remain so tight around my food issues was more painful than the risk to let go. Food was affecting my mood, sleep, energy – everything! I decided to embrace a new way: eating whole food, and enjoying it, without guilt.

And I'm guessing that you've had this moment, too, or a version of it. You've realised you get puffed out running after your kids. You find you can't fit into your favourite pair of jeans, the ones that make you feel like a rock star. You might feel tired and stressed after a hard day and find solace in wine and chocolate, until they make you feel sick and sad. Trust me, I've been there. I've had all those moments, but it wasn't until this moment – I call it 'the eyelash' – that I realised my life had to change. I might not have been dying, or obese, but I was done with my current lifestyle. I knew it wasn't making me happy, and I knew that I could change it. So I did – bit by bit, step by step.

That, my friends, is true shit. I am just like most of you reading this book: I have battled food. I have let it rule me. I have struggled to exercise. I've been the woman whose jeans won't do up, whose dress won't button at the back. I've been there. I get it. So when I say trust me, you can. Because I've done this, too. And because I've done it, I'm right here with you. We are in this together.

But why this book? I mean, why on earth would we need another 'diet' book? Another nutritionist telling you what to do and how to live? Another fad, another craze, one more thing to add to your to-do list… the one that never seems to shrink, no matter how many things you outsource or events you say no to.

First of all, I hear you. There are so many competing messages from different people – from qualified, experienced nutritionists like me, to doctors who deal with disease every day, to self-appointed wellness 'experts' (we'll get to them later). And, gosh, life is busy. In fact, it can be downright crazy sometimes. I know how long your to-do list is (it's probably at least as long as mine, and I deliberately hide mine so it doesn't haunt my dreams).

But you know what? That's exactly why we need this book: because life is busy and your to-do list will never get shorter. Because there are so many competing messages. We need this book because we need to cut through the crap and figure out how to eat again, in a way that supports, not strips, our health. And once we figure that out, we can get back to the business of life, in all its messy, busy, lovely glory.

But my guess is that you already know that (you're smart, I can tell). You know that there is a better way, but you need a little help. You're curious about how to eat well, still drink a little bit, and, along the way, lose some weight. You've come to the right place.

But first: if you're looking for a quick fix to lose four kilos in a week, this book is not for you. If you want to lose four kilos in a *month*, while maintaining a healthy, joyful, tasty but not super-strict lifestyle, then keep reading.

Like you, I want to be able to eat delicious food, have the odd glass of pinot and still feel great. I've written this book drawing on the latest research – and years of expertise and experience – to figure out what really works for the average busy person who wants to be healthy, but not in an extreme way. You want changes that are sustainable, and compatible with your life – not a seven-day detox or two days of bird food. Right?

We need this book because, while staying healthy is not overly complicated, it often seems as though it is. What's more, there are too many competing messages, too many complicated ways of framing nutrition and not enough evidence-based scientific data that underpins health. What I want to do is cut through the BS and show you how simple and straightforward living healthfully can be. You can eat, drink and – yes – still shrink, all while enjoying pinot and piccolos!

Why do we need this book? Three good reasons.

1 **Because there's too much 'white witchcraft' around**

How many of you have tried the Atkins diet? The Miami Beach Diet? The Lemon Detox Diet? Hands up if you've given the Breatharian Diet a go? It's so simple: just 18 hours of breathing only, followed by six hours of drinking nothing but fermented tea.

Okay, I'm kidding. There's no such thing as the Breatharian Diet (I hope not, anyway), but not a month seems to go by without another diet or nutritional fad popping up. Sure, there are some practical, well-researched nutritional approaches (and we will look at these), but many others have dubious health claims and are based on pseudo-science, at best.

During my nutrition studies, a lecturer warned us about 'white witchcraft': the almost deafening noise of so-called health information available, often free of charge, online, on social media and in magazines. While it's tempting to follow a detox plan by an Instagram wellness guru (they look so healthy, after all), there is a reason nutritionists get uni degrees in this stuff: it's important, it's complex and messing with your body too much can be dangerous.

So, how does the average person know what is true, and backed by evidence? It's hard. You might try a diet that gives you results and declare that it 'works'. Hey, you lost three kilos! But many such diets often require some type of restriction of calories or removal of a food group. Restrictive diets will work in the short term when you are in a state of starvation – i.e.

limited food, no fun. But as soon as you come off the diet, the weight returns. Then your mood slumps, along with your energy. And your self-esteem goes out the window because you didn't keep the weight off.

I'm not exactly sure how it happened but somehow, in this vast sea of Insta-famous wellness 'experts', I have become a Wise Woman of Health. It's how my publishers see me, and how people market me when I speak at their events. Initially I was a little confronted by this, but I now see that having years of life experience – not just as a nutritionist, but also as a mum, wife and corporate employee, and as someone who has witnessed illness, divorce, death and financial troubles – has given me a voice that is empathetic. I understand where you're coming from, because I have been there too. I've lived life. Not an Instagram-perfect life, but real life. And with this book, I'd love to share some of this wisdom with you.

2 **Because we need to go back to nourishment**

You know that rule about putting your own oxygen mask on first on a plane, before you put your kids' masks on? It applies to health, too. Taking care of yourself should not be a luxury, it should be something you do every day. Good nourishment should be tasty, easy, inexpensive and satisfying. It should be what fuels your energy, vitality, skin, immunity, brain health, sex life and more. And when you are fully nourished on a deep level, you can also nourish others a whole lot more.

Nourishment is not yo-yo dieting. It's not trying to fit into your jeans by Friday, or doing a juice cleanse because you've been 'bad' over the holidays. It's about eating real whole foods, and giving yourself permission to enjoy wine, coffee, chocolate – those little things that make life delicious.

When you make the transition to real, whole foods, your body and brain will feel satisfied. You will begin a lifetime of new habits. You'll be able to eat, drink and still shrink – or simply maintain your weight without obsessing about it! Finally, an opportunity to let go of guilt and bring in joy around food.

3 Because nutrition underpins everything

I believe most people want a few key things in their life:

- good relationships
- a feeling of happiness and contentment
- financial stability
- a sense of purpose and joy
- lots of energy and restorative sleep.

Does this sound good to you? It does to me.

But without proper nutrition, all these goals become very difficult to attain. If we do not eat well and fuel our bodies, other things – important things – fall by the wayside. For example, consider the following.

- **Good relationships** – If you're constantly exhausted from not eating well, or eating too much hidden sugar, how can you have the energy to create conversation and connection with other people?
- **Happiness** – If you're experiencing anxiety, depression or a mood disorder that may be connected to digestive issues or sugar highs and lows, how can you enjoy regular hits of happiness and genuine contentment?
- **Financial security** – Securing a good job requires a productive brain, fuelled by the nutrients in our food (especially good fats and slow carbs). Without these, we cannot function at our best.
- **Purpose and joy** – To find your purpose and to see joy, you need an open mind and clarity. If you're starving – or overstuffed – your brain is often foggy, without precision or mental stamina.
- **Energy and sleep** – Good energy requires sleep, which in turn requires limiting stimulants such as sugar, and consuming quality proteins that break down to tryptophan, the precursor to our sleep hormone melatonin.

So, nutrition is not just about eating well. Nutrition – eating healthfully, in a way that nourishes, not punishes – allows you to get on with your life, and live as fully as possible.

When good health becomes a habit, you are able to focus on other areas of your life and get on with the job of being your best self. And because you'll start to feel so much better about yourself, the effects will flow through to every part of your life.

You'll have better relationships, because you'll feel happy and contented within yourself. You'll feel stable and secure, and you'll probably do a better job at work with all your excellent new-found energy. You'll have an increased sense of purpose and joy, because your brain will be well nourished. You'll sleep better. You'll have better sex. You'll enjoy food more.

I could go on and on, but I think you get the point: good nutrition is good overall.

My Story:
A huge reality check

I would love to be able to tell you that if you eat well, sleep deeply every night and exercise moderately, life will reward you accordingly. Hey, a betting person would say your odds would be better than most, right?

It would be great if we could completely insure ourselves against disaster, but sometimes, no matter what we do and how healthy we are, life has other plans for us.

My brother, Greg, was six-foot-four and bulletproof. Greg was a firefighter in New York City, and was at the scene on that awful day, September 11, 2001. In fact, he was one of the very first responders. A real-life hero.

Greg was my little brother, but to me, he was larger than life. He had a great energy about him, and was one of those guys everyone is drawn to. Girls wanted to be with him and guys wanted to be like him. He was fit and funny and had a wickedly dry sense of humour. He had a fantastic wife, Lisa, and together they had two beautiful sons, Cooper and Ryder.

But like so many of those brave first responders, Greg suffered after 9/11. In 2014, he was diagnosed with lung cancer, as were many of the other firefighters and emergency workers exposed to the toxic conditions at Ground Zero. When I rushed back to New York to be with him, my nutritionist training kicked in. 'Greg!' I told him, 'I'll make you a green smoothie! You need a green smoothie!' Greg just laughed gently. 'Michele,' he said, 'I'm going to be dead in six months. I'm not drinking a green smoothie.'

Greg wasn't being facetious or even exaggerating. He was just being honest. The doctors hadn't given him long to live: only three months. To say our hearts were broken was an understatement. It was like someone telling you that everything you've ever known or believed in was totally wrong. It seemed unbelievable.

A few months later, I sat waiting with our cousin Billy, and Greg's best friend Pete, as Greg spoke to his doctor at the hospital. His brain was foggy from the chemo, and he couldn't keep the facts straight.

'Wait a minute,' he said. 'Are you saying I get to go home tonight?'

'Yes,' the doctor replied.

'Oh,' Greg said, struggling to understand. 'So when will they do the chemo again?'

The doctor paused. 'Greg,' she said. 'There's no more chemo. You can go home. You don't need to come back.'

'But when will they do the surgery?' Greg asked.

'Greg, there will not be surgery.'

Billy, Pete and I listened, trying to stem our tears as Greg heard his fate. He begged the doctor for a solution. Like us, he could not fathom that there was no solution.

My brother was wheeled out of the hospital that afternoon with a full salute by the medical team. The doctors thought that Greg wouldn't last another 48 hours, but somehow his will and New-York-firefighter spirit kept him with us for another 12 days. By then, he was barely a shadow of the man he'd been just 18 months prior.

I was broken when Greg died the day before his 43rd birthday. I didn't understand how someone so full of life was not here anymore. It took me a long time to accept that in life, there are simply no guarantees. You can live your life 'perfectly', healthy to a fault, and still fall victim to the cruelty of fate. Learning these lessons was pivotal, allowing me to frame 'health' in a different way.

Health should be about abundance, not deprivation. Pleasure, not punishment.

As Greg very well knew, green smoothies are great, but they have a time and a place. Life is short, and while we should take care of ourselves and nourish our bodies with good food and activity, we should also enjoy the heck out of life. And if that means a glass of wine or a piece of chocolate or a meal at a hatted restaurant where all bets are off, then I want you to go for it. Because life, my friend, is for living. Greg lived his life, all 43 years of it, to the fullest.

I'm trying to do that, too. I'd love you to join me.

1

What does your world look like?

Busy but deserving

The scene is pretty familiar: you've been up since 6 am when you put the washing on, then you race off to a spin class, rush back home to shower, put the dog outside with a bowl of water, feed the kids breakfast and make sure they are wearing matching socks. Somehow, in between all that, you gulp down a cup of coffee but forget to make yourself a bowl of oats as you make some for the kids.

Oh well, you think, there's always morning tea. But very quickly, your day is derailed by meetings and emails and last-minute changes to a presentation apparently only you can make. Then suddenly it's 3 pm and you've not only missed morning tea, but lunch as well.

So you have another coffee and think, I'd better have something to eat. Wanting to be healthy, you dig out an 'emergency' packet of fat-free jelly snakes from your desk drawer. You mean to eat just two – three, max – but end up scoffing down the whole packet, so by the time 5 pm rolls around you are both tired and wired. You've barely stopped all day, but you know what's going to greet you at home: dinner, tidying up, helping with homework and other chores.

Okay, you think, time for a wine. And maybe just a small packet of chips while you're making dinner.

After dinner, once you've packed the dishwasher and fed the dog, you realise you deserve another treat. So you reach into the freezer and pull out that tub of ice cream, and then it's only when you hear the spoon scraping against the bottom of the tub that you realise: damn, I've eaten the whole thing!

You go to bed feeling guilty and angry with yourself. I should have been stronger, you think. But the next day rolls around and you do it all over again…

The binge-eating cycle

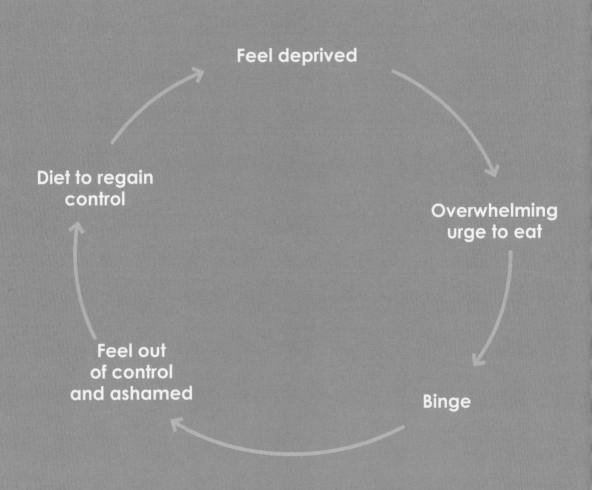

Feel deprived

Overwhelming
urge to eat

Binge

Feel out
of control
and ashamed

Diet to regain
control

It's 10 pm. You're just about to doze off when something takes over your thoughts. Did you put on the dishwasher? Damn. Did you order the voucher for your parents' wedding anniversary this weekend? Crap! You definitely forgot to register Jake for soccer…

Tired but wired

Now you're properly awake, because you've also just remembered, the budget deadline is Monday!

You probably know this scene pretty well. You'd give anything to sleep, except you're wide awake. You spend the next hour or two trying not to look at the clock, desperately counting sheep to get to sleep, yet still thinking about all the things you need to do.

The next day, you pay for it. You have that horrible, quasi-hungover feeling from lack of sleep, so you compensate with coffee and sugary treats.

That evening, you're so tired you think you might just fall asleep on the train home from work. You do – and then you can't sleep that night. And the cycle begins all over again.

What the hell is happening?

Why you can't sleep

There are three main reasons most people aren't sleeping well.

1. Too much sugar

You might be thinking, I barely touch sugar! And that may be true, but you'd be surprised just how much hidden sugar most of us consume during the course of a day, often in foods we assume are healthy because they're labelled 'organic' or 'vegan' or 'gluten-free'.

Excess sugar creates fluctuating blood-sugar levels, which in turn create fluctuating energy levels. This is what I refer to as the 'tired but wired' syndrome. Feeling exhausted at the end of the day, you innocently consume hidden sugar after dinner, and then suddenly feel wired again. Many of my clients would consume 'healthy lite' yoghurts before bed, not realising that they may have consumed more than 10 teaspoons of sugar in that small tub!

Also, having simple carbs that are full of sugar throughout the day delays your body's release of melatonin, the hormone that controls your sleep–wake cycle and helps you slide into deeper, higher-quality sleep.

So if you're not sleeping, perhaps sugar, hidden or otherwise, is the culprit. We'll look at sugar more closely in chapters 2 and 4.

2. Not enough protein

Eating on the run – 'grab and go' – usually means filling up on carbs. You know the drill: 'healthy' muffins, muesli bars, sandwiches, smoothies, pasta, crackers and takeaways.

Instead of filling our plates with vegetables, smart carbs and, most importantly, protein, we are being overfed but undernourished by hidden sugars and poor carb choices.

Our bodies need protein – found in eggs, meat, fish, legumes, dairy and tofu – because it contains an amino acid called tryptophan, which then converts to melatonin, our sleep hormone. So, eat an adequate amount of protein throughout the course of the day and you might just sleep easier. It's science, baby.

3. Out-of-control cortisol

Cortisol, commonly known as our 'stress hormone', wreaks havoc on sleep.

As healthy humans in a comfortable bed, we should be able to fall off to sleep easily within 30 minutes or so of lying down. If you can't do this, chances are your cortisol levels are an issue.

Later in this book we'll look at simple habits you can introduce to manage stress, nourish your body and once again start to enjoy nights of restful sleep.

The effects of disrupted sleep

A stressful day leads to our adrenal glands pumping excess cortisol all day long. Sadly, our stress hormone, cortisol, keeps pumping even when we hit the pillow for sleep. This does not make for a restful night's sleep at all.

And, unfortunately, a knock-on effect of lack of sleep, or continued poor sleep, can be weight gain or a resistance to weight loss. This is because lack of sleep can affect not only our sleep hormones but also our fat storage hormone, insulin. Sleep is a necessary human activity, and although its exact functions are still being researched, we do know that impairment in the duration of sleep is associated with worsened glucose tolerance, and even the development of insulin resistance and type 2 diabetes.

When our insulin becomes resistant or pre-diabetic, we can gain weight far too easily, no matter what we're eating or how much we exercise.

By keeping our stress levels in check, we will not only sleep better, we can take back control of our overall health.

The slimming secrets of sleep

THIS IS NOT 'FAKE NEWS'!

Sleep is more important to wellbeing than nutrition, exercise and connection. It really is the most important pillar of physical and mental health.

Why?

If you are not sleeping well, you are often not exercising or eating properly because you're so darn tired. And who wants connection when they are tired and cranky?

BUT SLIMMING, YOU SAY?

Quality sleep improves cellular repair, detoxification, brain clarity and even weight control. Lack of quality sleep can lead to a disruption in our fat storage hormone, insulin. When the job of insulin becomes sluggish, weight loss or even maintaining a healthy weight may become problematic. Approximately eight hours a night is a necessity, not a luxury, if you want to look and feel good.

SLEEP ESSENTIALS

 Keep your bedroom cool and as dark as possible.

 Clean your bedlinen regularly and replace old mattresses.

 Switch off screens at least 1 hour before bedtime.

 Don't consume caffeine or other stimulants in the evening.

 Get plenty of exercise, but don't exercise too close to bedtime as it will activate your stress hormones; leave at least 2–3 hours to wind down before bed.

STAYING ASLEEP

 Slow down your intake of water after 6 pm; waking to go to the toilet may catapult your mind into midnight 'monkey chatter'.

 Stress hormones like to hijack sleep. Find ways to reduce stress with daily meditation, breathing exercises and connection.

 Sugar is the enemy of sleep. Try to reduce your sugar intake. (Don't worry, you won't have this problem when following our 28-day plan!)

See pages 76–80 for more on the importance of sleep.

'I felt more
energetic; I started
walking through the
city at lunchtime,
something I haven't
done in years.'

The overworked IT guy

Donald Gleeson, 51, IT executive

'I've always been overweight. I was overweight as a kid, as a teenager, and I'm now an overweight 50-year-old man. All my life, I've tried to avoid discussing my weight as it embarrasses me. But over the past few years, I noticed that my list of medications was getting longer. At work, the guys in my office started talking about what cholesterol meds we were on, and comparing how many milligrams of blood pressure medication we were taking, and what we took for gout, and even sleep apnoea. I knew it wasn't healthy relying on medications, but it also didn't seem that bad – everyone was on them!

Then my bosses approached me after a board meeting and told me that my lifestyle and weight – I was, by that stage, 198 kilos – was putting the company at risk. Bam! That news rocked me completely. I thought I was too important to spend time getting healthy; the reality was that I was too important to not be healthy.

Michele has made this journey of weight loss so simple. She gets the struggle. She didn't judge me when I told her I drank 2 litres of Diet Coke every day. She gave me a plan to help me slowly cut back on it, and it really helped. I started eating more vegetables, and cut out bread and eventually, all carbs at night. My sleep improved immediately, and each week my pants became looser. I felt more energetic; I started walking through the city at lunchtime, something I haven't done in years.

I still have a long journey in front of me, but for the first time in ages I feel good. I am never hungry. My cholesterol and blood pressure moved into the healthy zone in eight weeks. And my pants keep getting looser.

I'm on my way, and this time I know I really can do it. The micro habits that Michele introduced were key – simple and achievable.'

Weighed down

So: we're overworked. Busy, tired, stressed. And many of us are overweight as a result.

Here's the hard truth: 63% of Australian adults are overweight or obese, along with one in four children and adolescents. We're not alone, of course – America and most other Western countries show similar statistics.

A real drag on our health

Besides the negative effects on our self-esteem, we know that obesity and excess weight can have major health effects, being major risk factors for conditions such as cardiovascular disease, high blood pressure, high cholesterol, metabolic issues, diabetes, insulin resistance and pre-diabetes.

Being overweight or obese also increases our risk of several cancers, including breast, bowel, kidney, liver, endometrial, ovarian, stomach, oesophagus, gallbladder, pancreas and prostate. In fact, being overweight or obese is the cause for nearly 4000 cancer cases in Australia each year.

We know this stuff, but have we also considered how being overweight or obese might impact our vitality, energy, productivity, self-esteem and more?

Let's talk about depression

Are you surprised to hear that being depressed is a risk factor for being overweight? Many people are – sometimes it's easy to overlook the link between our physical health and mental health.

Mental illness in Australia is all too common. One in five Australians aged 16–85 years will experience a mental illness in any one year. The most common mental illnesses are depressive, anxiety and substance-use disorder, and these often occur in combination.

While there are many factors at play when it comes to mental health, many of which we cannot predict or determine – from genetics to daily stresses to trauma – the one thing we can control is what we eat. More and more science is emerging that nutrition can be used as a preventive medicine for mental wellbeing. The SMILES trial, for instance, showed that a diet rich in fruit and vegetables, wholegrains and lean protein had a significant impact on reducing depressive symptoms. It's promising research, and I believe it's only the beginning.

My Story:
I was a human vacuum cleaner!

I haven't always been a nutritionist. Before that I was a marketing manager at Microsoft, juggling running a home with three kids, a dumb (but very cute) dog and a busy husband who travelled frequently for work. As they say in magazines, I had it all.

Except of course, I didn't. I existed on a not-very-fun cycle of stress–insomnia–starvation, and guess what? My weight see-sawed wildly. I swung between a size 10 and size 16, sometimes within weeks. It was unhealthy, to say the least, and rocked my self-esteem and confidence to the core. Whenever I put on weight, I would start the starving cycle again, but it would only make me gain more weight. Confused? I was too, until I started to look at what I was really doing to myself.

A typical day

Breakfast

**Two coffees.
Maybe even three.**

Lunch

**Salad (just enough
for a small bird),
hold the dressing.**

Dinner

**Fish and vegetables,
side order of smugness.**

Exercise

45-minute spin class.

I felt fantastic! Except, wait… no, I didn't. At around 2 pm, I'd start to get that brain fog where you try to remember a word and you just cannot locate it in your head.

By 3 pm I'd start to worry: is my iron low? Maybe it's my hormones making me feel this way? Is it menopause – at 29? Can that be possible?

At 3.30 pm I'd head to the bathroom just so I could have some relaxing alone time. Coming back to my desk, I'd pass the vending machine, and be almost overcome with the desire to buy everything inside. But I'd manage to walk past it, somehow, and return to my desk with nothing but a black coffee and a handful of Minties, thinking I was being 'good'.

By 9 pm, though, I'd be too tired to tell myself no – so I had the red wine, the chocolate biscuits, the cheese and crackers. I had it all.

My husband was right: I'd become a human vacuum cleaner.

And then, the next day, because I felt so terrible about the way I'd behaved the night before, I'd end up doing the same thing all over again.

Now for the good news

So here's the thing: deprivation is not health. Starving yourself, whether through force of will or because your day spirals out of control, will never work. Here's what does.

Loving food

Yes, loving food. I'm a nutritionist, and I love food! I love the way it tastes. I love the conversations around cooking, preparing and eating food. I look forward to a slice of birthday cake just as much as the next person. There is so much joy to be found in food: you only need look at the many ways we use food in cultural celebrations (hello, Christmas ham/fruit cake/pavlova!) to see this in action.

But when we deprive ourselves of food, we take away its joy. We see food as a means to an end – getting through the day with those fat-free jelly snakes, for example, or rewarding ourselves with an entire tub of ice cream at the end of the day.

Instead, what we need is a paradigm shift. By seeing food as something that nourishes us and makes us feel and look well, we can learn to enjoy it again.

Giving yourself permission to eat

This sounds simplistic, but it's important. You must tell yourself that it's okay – normal, healthy even – to eat and enjoy food.

I'm not talking about binge-eating a pizza. I'm talking about taking pleasure from the incredible flavours of real, whole foods and a glass of your favourite wine now and then.

Once you begin to eat well, without deprivation and starvation, the heightened appeal of 'naughty' foods will decrease, because you are satisfied and satiated by your food.

When you realise that you can eat, drink and still shrink without hunger pangs, mood swings, overly restrictive meals or tiny portion sizes, you will trust this process. You'll feel the proof in your body and the clarity in your head.

You won't have that 'Last Supper Syndrome' (a common experience among dieters on Sunday nights, preparing for Monday famines) and fixate on foods you can't have, because you'll be focused on the goodness you've added to your plate.

And you will be able to repeat this process daily because it's tasty, easy and achievable. It'll become a habit for life.

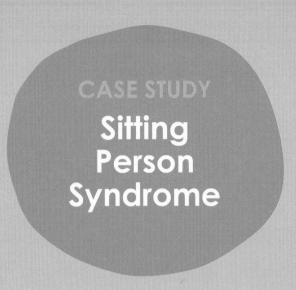

CASE STUDY

Sitting Person Syndrome

Mike Kallins, 22, uni student

'Like most uni students, I go out eating and drinking a lot, and when I'm not out, I'm sitting on my butt, studying. I put on a little weight in my last year of high school, but it was when I started uni that it really crept on. I would stay out late and then sleep in, realise I was going to be late to a lecture and grab something quick for breakfast, then lunchtime would roll around and I'd get what was offered at uni (cheap pasta, pizza or chips). By 4 pm I'd be so tired I'd need sugar to boost my energy.

When Michele first told me I'd be eating three meals a day, I thought, "There is no way I can fit three meals into my life every single day!" But my desire for change was greater than the obstacle in my head, so I gave it a go.

In three months, I dropped six kilos. I never felt hungry. It was weirdly wonderful. I stopped eating bread, ate three times a day, and snacked only occasionally – although most of the time I didn't need a snack as I was full from my meals. I also continued to go out with my mates for a drink now and then, and sometimes I even ate what I call "nasty food": junk.

Nowadays, I take my sleep seriously, and have stepped up my exercise routine to incorporate high-intensity interval training (HIIT). Michele taught me that healthy, successful people don't compromise on sleep or exercise, and now I know she's right.'

2

The absolute, ultimate, best diet ever

Gosh, I can just see you reading this, busting to find out what this 'best' diet is. Finally, an answer! Is it paleo? Keto? Vegan? Gluten-free? Fruitarian? Breatharian?

Nope. It's none of the above.

It's eating real food

Sexy, right? Rolls off the tongue. I just know it'll catch on.

Eating real, whole, unprocessed food as often as possible is the best thing you can do for your body and mind.

Eating a combination of quality fats (such as avocado, coconut oil and nuts), protein (eggs, nuts, tofu, meat) and complex carbs (brown rice, starchy vegetables, oats), as well as having the occasional treat such as a glass of wine, a bar of chocolate or a slice of pizza, will set you up on the path to good health for the rest of your life. That's it. Simple, huh?

So how could something that sounds so simple have become so difficult? I believe there are several reasons.

1. **We stopped believing.** Somewhere along the way, we stopped believing that food could be our medicine. But once you trust that good food and regular movement will benefit your physical and mental health, and you truly start to practise and believe this, it will become part of your daily life. A habit. You won't even think about it.
2. **We started restricting.** Eating well is not about cutting out foods for life. Many of us see nutrition as restricting: eating bland, tasteless foods or just starving ourselves. But that's simply not the case. Tasty, easy and affordable is my recommendation for food – if it isn't, you won't find it in this book. With small changes, we can achieve great things.
3. **We think it should be hard.** There seems to be a belief that eating healthily should be difficult. It's not. Absolutely not! For sure, eating well can take some getting used to, and you may need to make a few adjustments to your lifestyle. But these relatively small, simple changes will pay you back tenfold.
4. **We tell ourselves we're too busy.** Nourishing everyone else is easy; looking after ourselves can sometimes feel hard. But believe me, looking after everyone else is a lot easier when you're well rested, well fed, properly hydrated and productive.

Easy as F, P & CC

Creating a lifestyle with a diet that includes
a combination of fats, protein and complex carbs
is essential. Regardless of whether you're keto, paleo,
flexitarian or just carb-phobic, let me explain why
your body and brain needs these three essential
macronutrients. Understanding why you need certain
foods and having your own 'a-ha' moment will get you
one step closer to owning your own health plan.

F

Why we need FATS

Fat used to be one of the most feared words in the English language. Until relatively recently, low-fat and no-fat were the way to go. But, for the love of Nigella Lawson, please include fats in every meal. Yes, every meal.

There has been a massive shift in the way we think about fats. We used to think they caused a host of illnesses, from cardiovascular disease to diabetes and beyond. And while some fats – namely trans fats, often found in packaged cakes, muffins, crackers and processed foods – should definitely be off the menu, other fats, found in unprocessed foods, are actually good for you.

For starters, fats make food taste good. They also lower sugar cravings and help us feel full because they provide a signal to the brain to say, 'Hey, I'm satiated' (as anyone who's been on a no-fat or low-fat diet and felt hungry all the time will know all too well).

When we eat a diet rich in fats, it helps us 'crowd out' carbohydrates. This is because when we choose high-quality fats, protein and vegetables in a meal, we feel more satisfied, and as a result are less likely to reach for simple sugar-loaded carbs.

While there's still a lot of debate about saturated vs unsaturated fats in terms of our health, new research is showing that saturated fats are not the villains we once believed them to be. Dr Stephen Sinatra, one of the wisest integrative cardiologists of our time, states: 'The number one dietary contributor to inflammation in the artery walls is sugar. It's a far bigger threat than cholesterol. Reduce or, better yet, eliminate, sugar and processed carbohydrates in your diet and you reduce inflammation.'

My view is pretty straightforward. It doesn't take a rocket scientist to understand which fats are nourishing and which aren't. Tomato and goat's cheese salad, drizzled with extra virgin olive oil? Nourishing. Hot chips, glistening with oil? They might be tasty, but they're definitely not an everyday food.

FATS TO INCLUDE

Cold-pressed extra virgin olive oil; coconut oil, coconut milk; nuts and seeds; nut and seed oils, such as flaxseed, macadamia and walnut oil; olives; wild-caught fatty fish; avocados; grass-fed butter and ghee.

Why we need PROTEINS

Are you the type of person who's always grazing? A muesli bar here, a sugary biscuit there? If so, protein is going to be your new best friend.

When we eat protein at every meal, our blood sugar is stabilised and we feel full; we're not thinking about what we're going to eat next. As with 'good' fats, crowding out your meals with protein stops the desire for sugary post-meal snacks. Importantly, too, protein supports our immune system, builds lean muscle mass and plays an important role in the health of our skin, nails and hair.

PROTEINS TO INCLUDE

Eggs, fish, meat, cheese, dairy, legumes and tofu. Buy organic, grass-fed and local as often as you can, or buy the very best you can afford.

CC

Why we need COMPLEX CARBS

Yes, we really do need carbs! But we also need to be smart about them, which is why I call them 'smart carbs'.

If you've ever been on a low-carb or no-carb diet (keto, paleo and so on), you'll know that horrible feeling of fatigue and mental fog you can experience when you're deprived of smart carbs. Some people call this the 'keto flu' – they feel run down, irritable and just plain awful, with achy joints and bad breath. That's no way to live your life. Sure, there is a time and place for these diets – but not in this book, for the average busy person.

The truth is, both our brain and muscles prefer carbs as a fuel source – especially complex, slow-burning carbs such as brown rice, quinoa and oats, that provide us with fuel over a sustained period of time. The carbs we don't need? Anything white, sugary and overly processed: white bread, cakes, muffins and so on. These provide us with a short, sharp burst of energy – followed by a very steep crash.

'SMART' COMPLEX CARBS TO INCLUDE

Gluten-free sources: brown rice, quinoa, sweet potato, pumpkin, yams, buckwheat, millet, amaranth, basmati rice, corn, peas and carrots, as well as legumes (which are also a protein).

Gluten-containing sources: dark rye or grainy bread, spelt and oats.

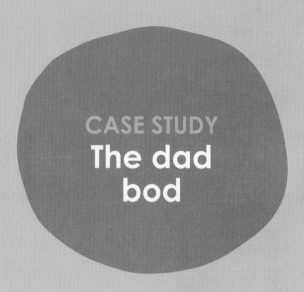

The dad bod

Christopher Stephinopolous, 54, solicitor

My daughters kept telling me I was getting a 'dad bod': that was the catalyst for seeing Michele. I thought I looked okay in my suit during the week, but it was on the weekends, when I was wearing shorts and T-shirts, that you could see what was really happening. My stomach stuck out, and so did my man boobs.

When I first visited Michele, she told me the cold hard facts. I weighed 101 kilos – 12 kilos more than when I got married. That was hard to swallow, but what was worse was that my visceral fat was in the dangerous zone, meaning I was at increased risk of cardiovascular disease. My dad had died of this when he was 54, so it was a huge wake-up call for me.

Within 12 months of seeing Michele and following her simple plan, I lost the 12 kilos I'd put on, reduced my visceral fat back into the healthy range, and had increased my lean muscle mass. No more man boobs!

The greatest surprise, though, was not my weight loss, but the difference in how I felt. I have more energy now than some of my colleagues who are in their 30s. See ya, dad bod.

'I have more energy now than some of my colleagues who are in their 30s.'

The truth about sugar & carbs

Now that you know smart carbs are good for our bodies, you might be thinking: how did we get this carb thing so wrong?

Many foods are sneaky sugar villains

While we all know there is a world of carbs that are no good for us and devoid of nutrition – soft drinks, packets of chips, sugary cakes, white bread, lollies and the like – I think we may be less aware of the sneaky carbs filling our tummies in other ways.

Some of us assume foods that are organic, vegan, gluten-free, dairy-free and wheat-free must therefore be healthy, but that's not always true. There are many products dressed up as healthy that are truly sugar villains. I'm thinking of those convenient 'grab and go' foods like 'lite' yoghurts, gluten-free muesli bars, protein balls and fat-free lollies that savvy marketers and manufacturers have led us to believe are healthy, simply because their labels claim the products are 'fat-free', 'all natural' or have 'no added sugar'. The packaging is sleek and shiny and makes us think, subconsciously, of good health. Smoothies are another good example. A popular berry smoothie with acai tells you it has real whole fruit and no gluten, corn syrup, fat, artificial flavours or preservatives – but what it doesn't tell you is that it also contains 22 teaspoons of sugar! Now some of that sugar will be from the berries, but sneakily they don't disclose the word sugar, calling it 'sherbet' instead.

In fact, many or even most of these 'grab and go' foods are highly processed and packed with sugar, salt and empty carbs. And these are just the carbs that look like they're good for us!

It all adds up, baby!

How much sugar do you eat in an average day? A teaspoon? Maybe two? Hmmm. My bet is that you consume a lot more sugar than you think you do. The WHO states that, for maximum health, we shouldn't be consuming more than 6 teaspoons of added sugar per day.

Guess what? Many of us eat more than 30 teaspoons of added sugar every single day. I see this in my clinical practice daily, and clients are so surprised when we run through what they are used to eating each day. Dairy, fruit and vegetables all contain natural sugars – but it isn't natural sugars that we are overly concerned with. It is the added sugars like white or brown sugar, corn syrup and maple syrup that are detrimental to our health.

If you're thinking, how the heck does anyone eat 30 teaspoons of sugar a day, then consider this: a can of soft drink has 10 teaspoons of added sugar, a fruit smoothie has 22 teaspoons, and banana muffins (which now are the size of a doorstop) might have 15 teaspoons. Now think of all the other foods we're eating regularly that contribute to our daily sugar intake – slices, cakes, muesli bars, cereals, protein bars, flavoured yoghurts – and it's not hard to see how we get to those 30 teaspoons daily.

You don't need to be a nutritionist to understand that this much sugar simply isn't good for us.

THE POTENTIAL LONG-TERM EFFECTS OF A HIGH-SUGAR DIET INCLUDE:

- insulin resistance
- weight gain that is hard to reverse
- hormonal imbalance
- inflammation

We need to ask ourselves – are we having a mood swing, or is it just a 'sugar swing?'

The sugar roller-coaster

The not-so-sweet side of the sugar rush

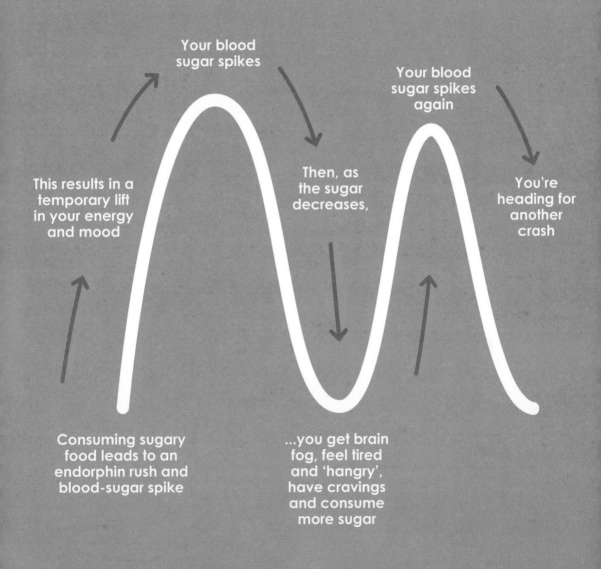

Your blood
sugar spikes

Your blood
sugar spikes
again

This results in a
temporary lift
in your energy
and mood

Then, as
the sugar
decreases,

You're
heading for
another
crash

Consuming sugary
food leads to an
endorphin rush and
blood-sugar spike

...you get brain
fog, feel tired
and 'hangry',
have cravings
and consume
more sugar

The consequences of excess sugar

Sugar gives us energy, but in excess it can be harmful to our brain and body. It gives us a quick spike of fuel, followed by a big dip in energy – something you'll be familiar with if you've ever eaten a big bowl of pasta and then immediately wanted to take a nap. Here are three ways excess hidden sugar might be playing havoc with you.

Hormone health

For healthy hormones, our bodies need proper nourishment. Too much sugar can throw the following hormones out of whack.

* **Thyroid hormones** – these govern our metabolism. Our thyroid gland needs iodine, selenium, vitamin B12, zinc and a good nutrient supply to keep it working properly. Packaged and processed foods that are packed with sugar often lack these nutrients.

* **Insulin** – our fat storage hormone. To keep our insulin levels in check, we need to keep our intake of added sugars low. Excess sugar consumption leads to excess glucose, and when this isn't burnt for energy and accumulates repeatedly, it can lead to insulin resistance or pre-diabetes and makes weight loss very difficult.

* **Cortisol** – this is our stress hormone, which is governed by our adrenal system, and dislikes sugar overload. Food itself doesn't contain cortisol, but sugary foods can raise cortisol levels to more than a healthy body requires. Excess cortisol affects our immune system and digestion, and reduces levels of our calming hormone, progesterone.

2

Brain health

None of us wants to feel like we have a 'broken' brain, and yet many of us do experience poor brain function, at least occasionally – from 'brain fog', lack of concentration and poor memory, to anxiety or depression.

The good news is that eating whole, real food – packed with fats, protein, smart carbs and fibre, and low in added sugar – is like fertiliser for the brain. If we keep our blood sugar from wildly fluctuating up and down, we'll have the energy we need to think, process information and make decisions. And if we regularly eat high-quality fats, we can dampen inflammation throughout the body – a key culprit in brain dysfunction.

3

Mental health

Depression is silent, scary and has many causes. And while depression and mood disorders may be linked to factors largely outside our control, such as genetics, disease and external stressors and toxins, the one thing we can control is what we eat, and we know there is a link between food and mood.

As we saw earlier, studies are increasingly showing the important role good nutrition plays in our mental wellbeing, with the gold-standard SMILES trial on major depression concluding: 'dietary improvement may provide an efficacious and accessible treatment strategy for the management of this highly prevalent mental disorder'.

Eating real, unprocessed foods benefits not only our body, but our mental health. Too much sugar is bad news for our mood.

Is it because sugar-laden foods are often devoid of nutrients we need for biochemical pathways that create our happy hormones?

Is it because sugar creates dysbiosis in the gut, or symptoms such as irritable bowel, and it is our gut that creates 90 per cent of our happy neurotransmitter, serotonin?

Is it because clean, whole foods are full of vitamin B, and this gives us energy, which has a flow-on effect to everything we do in life?

Probably all of the above. Meanwhile, research continues at a rapid pace in the area of nutritional psychiatry.

But what about 'natural' sugar?

So here's the thing: our brain and body love glucose as a source of energy. Sure, our body can run off the energy we get from fat and protein alone, but for busy productive people, smart carbs allow us to function exceptionally well.

Sweet potatoes, pumpkin, beetroot, carrots, quinoa, brown rice, buckwheat and oats: these kinds of complex carbs break down into natural sugars that our body can then use for creative thinking, critical skills, decision-making and concentration. Smart, natural carbs also keep our muscles energised, fuelled up and ready to move.

Put simply, the sugars naturally occurring in dairy, fruit and vegetables are fine. These sugars – lactose in dairy, and fructose and glucose in fruits and vegetables – are naturally occurring and provide us with energy. Some of these foods have a lower sugar count than others, so if you want to lose weight, stick to those low in sugar. And by sticking to whole foods – full-fat plain yoghurt, for example, or an apple with the skin on, for the all-important fibre – you can't go too far wrong. Of course, if you have issues with the lactose in dairy (bloating, constipation, diarrhoea or abdominal discomfort), give dairy a miss.

The final word on sugar

1. The sugar naturally occurring in fresh whole fruit is fine. If you are wanting to lose weight, stick to low-sugar fruits like berries, eat a maximum of two serves a day and enjoy them.

2. Know the difference between starchy and non-starchy vegetables. Starchy vegetables are solid and heavy – potatoes, sweet potatoes, pumpkin and so on. Eat them earlier in the day so your body has a better chance of metabolising their natural sugars. At night, stick to non-starchy, more water-based vegetables. Refer to the list on page 135.

3. If in doubt, crowd it out. When your meals are packed with protein, healthy fats and non-starchy vegetables, you'll find you don't have much cause to reach for refined carbs and sugary snacks.

Give hidden sugars the flick

To stop those sneaky added sugars creeping into your diet, follow these three simple steps.

1. **Look at the food label.** If you can read, pronounce and understand all the ingredients, go to step 2. If the ingredients sound like a whole bunch of chemicals, they probably are – so ask yourself: do I really, really want this? After all the time, money and effort you spend on facials, haircuts, clothes and gym memberships, do you really want to foil your efforts by eating junk?

2. **Check the serving size on the nutrition panel.** Sometimes manufacturers make the serving size tiny to disguise the amount of sugar in the food. For instance, you might assume a chocolate bar is simply one serving, but check the nutrition panel and you might find it serves two. If you look only at the amount of sugar in the product, and not the serving size, you might assume it has far less sugar than it really does. And don't get caught out by cereal manufacturers who say a 'serving' is the size of a shot glass. When they do this, you can be sure the product is loaded with sugar!

3. **Check the sugar count.** Look at how many grams of sugar are in the food. To work out roughly how many teaspoons this equates to, divide that number by four. For instance, let's say one small tub of honey-flavoured yoghurt has 30 grams of sugar. One teaspoon of sugar is about 4 grams – so if you divide 30 grams by four, you'll see there's around 7 teaspoons of sugar in that tub of yoghurt. It's not an exact science, but it's a good way to quickly eyeball food and see if it's worth eating.

Manufacturers know we're a savvy bunch. They know we know sugar isn't great for us – so they've come up with a whole list of aliases for sugar, to try to sneak it into products without you realising. Turn to page 215 for more information.

'I've created new habits: eating three times a day, packing my meals with lots of protein and vegetables.'

CASE STUDY
The fresh start

Janelle Gaynor, 49, human resources expert

'This sounds crazy, but I think my sugar addiction caused my divorce. I'm not kidding. I was addicted to food, and sugar in particular. For six years, I depended on food in an extremely unhealthy way. I ate high-carb, nutritionally empty foods that sent me on a physical and emotional roller-coaster. I was constantly exhausted. I became a loner because I had no self-confidence.

I was so embarrassed by the state of my entire being when I met Michele, but she immediately put me at ease. She said, "You are not allowed to beat yourself up anymore. You can't fail at good nutrition; if you stuff up, you just pick up at the next meal. End of story."

I've never met anyone like Michele. Not only did her advice make sense, but she knew exactly how I felt. She's been in my shoes, and knows the pain of disliking yourself. It's a horrible feeling.

Over the past 18 months I've lost 17 kilos. I still eat dark chocolate and enjoy a cab sav a few nights a week. I've created new habits: eating three times a day, packing my meals with lots of protein and vegetables. I never miss a meal – why would I, when everything I've learned to cook is easy and delicious? One of the loveliest things is that I now cook once a month for my book club, a group of like-minded women who I'm thrilled to call my friends. Even better, I finally feel like I am worthy of this tribe.'

The lowdown on fruit

Summer just wouldn't be summer without punnets of fresh berries and sweet, juicy mangoes. It wouldn't be autumn without poached pear on my morning porridge, or crisp apples in my fruit bowl. Fruit makes an excellent snack, can be added to salads and other meals, and offers natural sweetness when we need it.

But when you are trying to reduce your sugar intake, it's important to pay attention to the fruit in sugar, known as fructose. Some fruits contain quite a lot of fructose, and others very little.

Here's a list of fruits ranked from high to low on the sugar index to help you navigate the fresh fruit aisle at the supermarket. Each serving is 1 cup for ease of comparison.

I've also included the fibre content in grams. Ideally, you want a high fibre count and low sugar count.

The fibre in fruit helps blunt the blood sugar spikes. So, for example, if you drank the juice of four apples (with no added sugar) it would make your blood sugar swing the same way a can of cola would. But if you ate four whole apples, with their skins on for fibre, your blood sugar spike would be a lot less dramatic. The less dramatic the blood sugar swing, the more even energy and brain clarity we have.

Have a look to see how your favourite fruit ranks.

FIGS
Total Sugar: 29.3 g
Fibre: 5.2 g

POMEGRANATE SEEDS
Total Sugar: 23.8 g
Fibre: 7.0 g

MANGO
Total Sugar: 22.5 g
Fibre: 2.6 g

TANGERINES
Total Sugar: 20.6 g
Fibre: 3.5 g

BANANAS
Total Sugar: 18.3 g
Fibre: 3.9 g

SWEET CHERRIES
Total Sugar: 17.7 g
Fibre: 2.9 g

PLUMS
Total Sugar: 16.4 g
Fibre: 2.3 g

PINEAPPLE
Total Sugar: 16.3 g
Fibre: 2.3 g

KIWIFRUIT
Total Sugar: 16.2 g
Fibre: 5.4 g

GRAPEFRUIT
Total Sugar: 15.9 g
Fibre: 3.7 g

APRICOTS
Total Sugar: 15.3 g
Fibre: 3.3 g

GRAPES
Total Sugar: 15.0 g
Fibre: 0.8 g

BLUEBERRIES
Total Sugar: 14.7 g
Fibre: 3.6 g

ORANGES
Total Sugar: 14.0 g
Fibre: 3.6 g

HONEYDEW MELON
Total Sugar: 13.8 g
Fibre: 1.4 g

PEARS
Total Sugar: 13.7 g
Fibre: 4.3 g

APPLES
Total Sugar: 13 g
Fibre: 3 g

PEACHES
Total Sugar: 12.9 g
Fibre: 2.3 g

NECTARINES
Total Sugar: 11.3 g
Fibre: 2.4 g

ROCKMELON OR CANTALOUPE
Total Sugar: 9.4 g
Fibre: 0.6 g

WATERMELON
Total Sugar: 9.4 g
Fibre: 0.6 g

STRAWBERRIES
Total Sugar: 7.4 g
Fibre: 3.0 g

BLACKBERRIES
Total Sugar: 7 g
Fibre: 7.6 g

RASPBERRIES
Total Sugar: 5.4 g
Fibre: 8.0 g

CRANBERRIES
Total Sugar: 4.3 g
Fibre: 3.6 g

A NOTE ON DRIED FRUIT

Dried fruit is very high in sugar, so it's best enjoyed only as a very occasional snack. Avoid buying muesli with dried fruit, and add your own fresh fruit instead when serving. Dried fruits are great in baking, as their intense flavour packs a sweet punch, meaning a small amount goes a long way!

Ditch those scales

While we're busy sorting fact from fiction, let's get another thing straight. Don't get caught up by the number on your bathroom scales. DON'T.

Scales measure gravity, not your wellbeing. That is the absolute truth. The scales simply show your weight, based on how much force is being applied by your body to the earth. That's it. The number they register is not a true reflection of your vitality, energy, passion, spirit and kind heart. If your bathroom scales measured all of these, I would endorse weighing yourself regularly – but they don't. So don't weigh yourself every day.

Why numbers don't stack up

1. Did you know your weight fluctuates daily, based on factors such as water retention, your hormone cycle, and when you last went to the toilet? So those numbers on the bathroom scale are not a great way to measure weight loss.

2. When we're on one of those old-school diets where we count calories and obsess about cutting down on what we eat, we spend 90 per cent of our time obsessing about 10 per cent of our weight. Imagine all the time you've wasted beating yourself up, rather than acknowledging the good things about yourself, all in pursuit of that number on the scale. Ironically, most of us who are concerned with our health naturally drop weight when we stop obsessing over that number on the scales. When we allow ourselves to eat and drink moderately, without tightly controlled boundaries, we begin to shrink. It's deprivation that makes us 'hangry' (a state of hunger stemming from anger), which eventually makes us binge and sends our self-esteem plummeting again.

If you really need some stats

If you really want to track evidence of weight loss, invest in a set of bio-impedance scales and measure yourself no more than twice a week.

Bio-impedance scales measure not just your overall weight, but your percentage of water, lean muscle mass and fat, your bone density and, importantly, your percentage of visceral fat, the dangerous fat that sits around your internal organs.

A good habit to get into is to weigh yourself only on Monday and Friday mornings. Weigh yourself when you first get up, with no clothes on, after you go to the toilet but before you drink your first glass of water. I recommend Monday and Friday weigh-ins because it's relatively easy for most of us to stay in the moderate zone of eating and drinking from Sunday night to Thursday night, so these two weigh-ins are more likely to give you an accurate view of your overall wellbeing over the course of the week, and will help keep you on track.

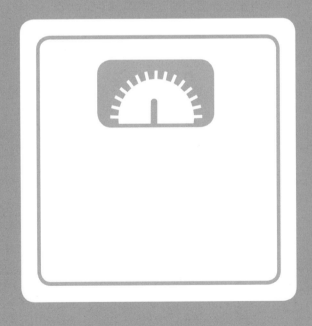

CASE STUDY
The party girl

Felecia Toppan, 40, small business owner

'I am a party girl. I always have been and always will be. I love coffee and champagne. In my 20s, I got away with my love of food and drink, but in my 30s, after having two kids, I became one of those people who only had to look at food to put on weight. I gained eight kilos and felt bloated, puffy and constantly exhausted. Even starving myself and doing juice cleanses didn't budge the scales. They only left me more exhausted.

A friend told me about Michele, and as soon as I started her plan, I began to shrink. I couldn't understand what was happening. I was eating so much, and still losing weight! I learned that if I removed the carbs and replaced them with good fats and proteins, I'd feel full, and the weight would drop off. It was a revelation.

Today, I'm not skinny: I'm healthy. It's true that I'll always be a party girl, but now I have the skills to navigate my nightlife. I can still drink my bubbles and have my dark chocolate without feeling guilty and starting from zero again.'

'It's true that I'll always be a party girl, but now I have the skills to navigate my nightlife.'

Diet myths, busted

MYTH #2
Eating low-fat food will make me lose weight.

THE TRUTH: The best weight-loss diet is a wholefood plan that you can stick to because you feel nourished. One that is so satisfying, tasty and doable that it becomes a habit. I am not a fan of skim- or low-fat products, because eating healthy fats creates a feeling of satiation, not deprivation.

MYTH #1
Drinking diet soft drink will help me lose weight. It hasn't got any sugar!

THE TRUTH: New research suggests that drinking artificially sweetened drinks is associated with diabetes. A 2018 study at the University of Texas, presented at the American Diabetes Association, added to growing research that consumption of diet soda was associated with diabetes and metabolic syndrome, and that aspartame exposure may directly contribute to an increase in blood glucose levels. I see this in our clinic practice weekly. Even if a client does nothing more than get rid of their addiction to diet soft drinks, they lose weight!

GF

MYTH #3
Gluten-free means it's healthy.

THE TRUTH: Sure, eating gluten-free food is good if you're coeliac or sensitive to gluten. However, there's now a whole raft of packaged foods labelled as gluten-free that don't resemble real, whole foods in the slightest. If you experience pain or discomfort when eating gluten, by all means look for alternatives. If you don't, stick to the unprocessed version of that food.

MYTH #4
Eating five meals a day is best for everyone.

THE TRUTH: Everyone is different. While five small meals a day might work for your colleague, you might feel satisfied with three normal-sized, nutrient-dense meals. I often find that once my clients start crowding out their meals with protein, fat and non-starchy vegetables, their snack cravings all but disappear.

MYTH #6
Supplements help weight loss.

THE TRUTH: There is a time and place for good quality supplements, but not when trying to lose weight. They might work in the short term, but they're not a solution for wellbeing. You know what is? Eating real food, sleeping well and getting active.

MYTH #7
Your weight is a measurement of good health.

THE TRUTH: Your weight is one measurement of good health, sure. But it's not the be-all and end-all. When assessing a person's overall health, we also need to consider their sense of vitality and energy, their general mood, as well as their sense of connection and restedness. Health is complex and we can't sum it up with one simple number.

MYTH #5
Eating carbs makes you fat.

THE TRUTH: Sure, eating too many carbs doesn't help weight loss. But eating smart carbs – the kinds we've talked about already – helps sustain energy. If weight loss is a goal, try having a low-carb dinner.

MYTH #8
Exercise will keep you slim.

THE TRUTH: You can't exercise your way out of a bad diet. Many of you will immediately know what this means. You run 10 kilometres every day to make up for the 'bad' night you had with burgers, chips and beers. Or you simply exercise excessively just so you can eat anything you want. This is a form of punishment – not enjoyable exercise.

MYTH #10
Avoid all sugar – even the fructose in fruit.

THE TRUTH: Fruit in its whole form – not juiced – is one of life's gifts. Whole fruit provides us with antioxidants and fibre, and is delicious! Enjoy, as with all things, in moderation.

MYTH #9
You must eat superfoods every single day.

THE TRUTH: 'Superfood' is a marketing term. Stick to real, whole, unprocessed food and trust me, you'll be eating a diet packed with superfoods.

MYTH #11
Eating lots of eggs is bad for you.

THE TRUTH: Eggs used to be demonised because their yolks contain high amounts of cholesterol. But it's since been found that the cholesterol in eggs has no bearing on our blood cholesterol.

MYTH #12
Eating red meat is unhealthy.

THE TRUTH: If you like red meat, enjoy it once or twice a week without concern. Buy grass-fed and organic as much as possible, which are both better for the animal and for you.

MYTH #14
Breakfast is the most important meal of the day.

THE TRUTH: Did your mother tell you this, too? It's a nice idea, but if you don't like to eat a morning meal, don't force yourself. Some people like to fast before lunch, and that's fine if it feels good to you.

MYTH #15
Doctors know everything.

THE TRUTH: Nope. Only nutritionists know everything. Ha! No, of course this is untrue. But seriously, health professionals are always learning, as new evidence emerges. So listen, learn and adapt, and trust your intuition just as doctors (and nutritionists!) do.

MYTH #13
Juice cleanses are a good way to detox your body.

THE TRUTH: Your body does a great job of detoxifying itself, using a handy organ known as the liver. A simple whole-food cleanse that doesn't include alcohol and only a small bit of caffeine is often a welcome 'cleanse' to reset after holidays. But if you do undergo a juice cleanse, you'll most likely binge when you're done, because you've effectively starved yourself. Stick to real food and nourish, not punish.

So where
do we start?
Small.

Most behavioural
psychologists agree
that it's difficult to
create a whole raft
of new habits all at
once. So, we're going
to start by making
a few simple
micro changes.

I actually prefer the term 'micro habits', because small sustainable changes, done daily, soon become entrenched habits.

We're not going to set our sights on losing five kilos in a week; that's unrealistic and will only set you up for failure. But what about losing 250 grams in a week? Could you do that? (Yep, you sure could.) And if you did that every week for a whole year, you'd lose 12 kilos. How does that sound?

Over the next 28 days, I want you to choose three micro habits that will help you become healthier. After four weeks, when you have these habits thoroughly incorporated into your daily life, you can choose three more.

My first 3 micro habits

When I began my own wellbeing journey, I chose to work on sleep, hydration and sugar in my first month.

1. I went to bed a little earlier. Instead of going to bed at 10.30 pm, I went to bed at 9.45 pm. It's not a massive change, so I was able to stick with it. (A much harder change would've been going to bed at 9 pm.)

2. I started each day by drinking a glass of water. And about 45 minutes before each meal, I had another one. I didn't set some goal like 'I must have 3 litres of water a day'; I just reminded myself a lot more often that water was important.

3. I stopped eating foods that contained added sugar. Instead, I started eating far more real foods. No more muesli bars, fat-free lollies, flavoured yoghurts and packaged junk foods, and more fruits, vegetables and full-fat dairy.

Those micro habits turned out to be pretty easy – not at all painful. So I did them day after day, and pretty soon, they were just things I did naturally, without thinking about them. Once I felt I could do these ones, I added more small changes. And so on, and so on.

As my de-bloated body and de-fogged brain began to feel better and better, I found it was easy to keep crowding in these achievable changes.

Now, what will you change? Go on, write them down. Science tells us what we write down and see we can more easily incorporate into our daily life. Many of my clients will take three sticky notes and place them on their bathroom mirror to read every morning. I still do this, then I take a photo and use it as my screensaver. When I am ready to move on and add a few more, I repeat the process.

3

How to get it right in your world

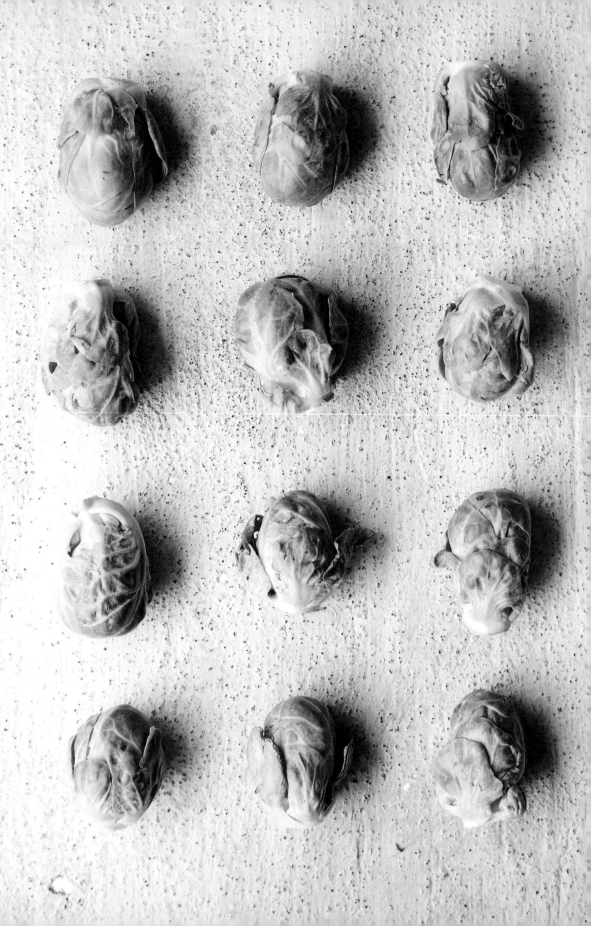

By now, we know what your typical day looks like. But what about your ideal day? A day where most things go well, and you make healthy sustainable choices that fuel your energy, rather than sap it? What does that day look like?

My ideal day

6 am: *Wake-up, drink a glass of water and go to the toilet.*

6.45–7.30 am: *Exercise. Three mornings a week, I do HIIT (high-intensity interval training), on another two mornings I do a group exercise class (a combination of cardio and weights), and on the other two mornings I practise yoga or go for a walk. Yes, I move every single day.*

7.30 am: *Time for more water, and a coffee. I love a piccolo latte or a ¾ double shot cappuccino.*

7.45–9 am: *Shower, then breakfast. I try to plan my breakfast the night before, and I encourage you to do this, too. The more prep you can do the night before, the better! If I'm roasting vegetables for my kids, I'll roast a few more and set them aside for my breakfast. I love heating a leftover roast sweet potato and topping it with wilted spinach, scrambled eggs, some avocado, a dash of olive oil and a sprinkle of flaxseeds. It sounds indulgent but it's done in five minutes.*

9 am: *Time to head to the office. I fill up my favourite water bottle and have it on my desk, to sip throughout the day. It might sound silly but having my favourite bottle nearby really does make me drink more water. Try it!*

10.30 am: *My first big cup of tea for the day. I love English Breakfast, but often I go for a herbal tea like Bengal Spice from Celestial Seasonings or Black Adder Liquorice from Red Seal (they're really good for reducing sugar cravings). If I'm hungry, I'll have a handful of nuts (any kind) but mostly I find that my breakfast, with its combination of smart carbs, protein and fat, is enough to tide me over until lunch.*

11.30 am–12.30 pm: *As I'm working, I make sure I drink lots of water infused with lemon, lime, mint or any fruit I have in the kitchen or office bench. This helps me reduce mindless snacking; so many people confuse hunger for thirst.*

1 pm: *Lunchtime! Like many, I'm time-poor in the middle of my working day, and I hate wasting money. For lunch, then, I plan ahead and make a double (or even triple) batch of my evening meal, and add a small amount of smart carbs. One day might be savoury turkey meatballs (page 154), to which I'll add ½ cup cooked brown rice or quinoa. Or I might make an extra serve of the pancetta frittata on page 188 and serve it with a slice of dense rye bread.*

I try to eat lunch outdoors for a hit of vitamin D, and I take my time, too – at least half an hour, sometimes 45 minutes if I can. My mornings are either noisy with people's requests, or just noisy in my own head, so lunch is a chance to switch off. After I eat, I either go for a short walk or tune into a meditation or breathing app on my phone. Tuning back into myself allows me to tune into other people better when I am back at my desk.

1.45 pm: *Meetings, emails and more.*

3.30 pm: *Afternoon tea. I have a big drink of water, a cup of tea and some plain full-fat Greek-style yoghurt (topped with nuts, seeds or shredded coconut, and sometimes a hit of vanilla bean paste). I take a moment to check out by calling my husband, kids or a friend, stretching or having a short walk, even just around my office.*

5–6 pm: *Quittin' time! I stop at the shops (to pick up what I forgot on the weekend). When I get home, I make dinner while chatting to the kids. While I'm cooking, I'll have a glass of sparkling water, or maybe a glass of pinot noir. I turn off my phone so I'm present, listening, engaged — and not multitasking.*

---

7 pm: *I try to eat at 7 pm, so that I can have a gap of at least 12 hours before I eat again in the morning.*

Dinner is mostly a combination of quality protein, good fats and lots of non-starchy vegetables. As a family, we all eat the same meal, but for the kids I'll sometimes add more starchy vegetables or smart carbs (the same ones I then use for my breakfast or lunch the next day). I might have another glass of wine — it's nice to unwind after a day at work. But I stop at two, and try to always give myself two wine-free nights a week.

And one night a week, I practise one of my favourite micro habits that has become a simple habit, with key benefits for my waistline: intermittent fasting. That's right — no dinner at all. Sometimes I may have a cup of vegetable or bone broth, or a cup of tea, but that's it. I give my body a break, and it really likes it. We'll explore this further on page 125.

9.30 pm: *Bedtime. For at least one hour before I go to bed, I try not to have blue light from my computer or phone near me. It winds me up and has been scientifically proven to reduce melatonin production, which interferes with quality sleep.*

Phew. So that's me. Now I want you to think about what your ideal day looks like. What do you want to achieve? What are your micro habits, and how will you incorporate them into your daily routine? How will you account for setbacks?

Your ideal day

Now it's your turn. Take a moment to think through what a healthy day looks like to you, and write your thoughts below. Ask yourself: what do I need to do to make that day a reality?

Morning

_____

_____

_____

_____

_____

_____

_____

_____

_____

_____

_____

_____

Afternoon

_____
_____
_____
_____
_____
_____
_____
_____
_____

Evening

_____
_____
_____
_____
_____
_____
_____
_____
_____

Embrace the beauty of micro habits

In order to live well – in good health, with adequate energy and vitality to live our best lives, and to be able to eat, drink and still shrink – there are some things we cannot compromise on. Some things we just need to do, every single day. We need sufficient rest. We need to drink water to stay hydrated. We need to consume nourishing foods to fuel our brain and body. We need to move. We need to look after our mental health and sense of connectedness.

Some people would simply call these things 'self care', and I see how that label fits.

I call them my 'non-negotiables': micro habits I need to pay attention to, so that I can get on with the job of being me.

The great thing is, these micro habits are not difficult to do, but the difference they'll make to your life can be enormous.

You can fit them into your daily life almost immediately – and, even better, they will help support your overall health goals, which means you can still enjoy those little indulgences that make life so pleasurable: good coffee, chocolate, wine, champagne, a bit of pizza every now and then.

Sound good? Then let's get started.

My non-negotiable

#1

SLEEP

Do not compromise on sleep. We all know that lack of sleep makes us grumpy and foggy, but did you know how much it impacts on your waistline, and your health generally?

Most of us have experienced a few nights of inadequate sleep, and know all too well how it makes us look old and tired. Our skin becomes sallow and pale, our eyes swell, dark circles appear and our wrinkles deepen.

When we don't sleep enough, our bodies also release more of our stress hormone, cortisol. When cortisol is released, it breaks down collagen, the protein in our skin that helps give it that lovely firm appearance.

Sleep could also be the culprit if you're struggling to lose or maintain your weight. A recent study with over 200 participants undergoing a sleep-restricted week showed that sleep deficiency is linked to weight gain. After only a week, participants who slept just four hours a night gained an average of one kilo, compared to those who slept as much as they wanted to. Many similar studies have offered up the same conclusion – that weight and sleep are deeply intertwined.

What's happening when we don't sleep

When our bodies are robbed of sufficient good-quality sleep, our biochemistry goes haywire. Two hormones in particular get a little crazy.

Leptin

Everyone's talking about leptin, also known as the 'appetite hormone'. When leptin is working properly, it sends a signal to the brain to say 'Hey buddy, no more cake – you're full now.' We all need this reminder to get us to put our forks down. But, unfortunately, the less sleep we have, the less leptin we create. And when we don't have enough leptin, we don't have that inner voice telling us when we've had enough.

Insulin

Our fat storage hormone, insulin, can become resistant when we aren't getting adequate sleep. Sleep deprivation also increases production of cortisol, which can make cells more resistant to insulin. Poor sleep can also trigger changes to thyroid hormones and testosterone, which can lead to decreased insulin sensitivity and higher blood glucose, which in turn leads to weight issues.

Micro habits for good sleep

- **Restructure your bedtime.** Start going to bed a little earlier every night, but make this change slowly. If you normally fall asleep at 11.30 pm, don't try to get into bed tonight at 9 pm. Gradually move your bedtime earlier by 15 minutes until you're in bed by 10 pm. If you know you need more sleep than this (like me!), try to eventually be in bed by 9.30 pm.
- **No blue light after dinner.** No computer, no phone, no laptop – or as little as possible, anyway (nobody's perfect). Make your bedroom a sanctuary: keep it clean, tidy, cool and dark, and you'll find you sleep so much better.
- **Eat good 'sleep food'.** Too much sugar creates 'monkey chatter' in our mind and leads to poor sleep. Keep added sugar to a minimum, and eat protein at each meal to keep hunger and sugar cravings at bay. Protein also breaks down to an amino acid called tryptophan, which is the precursor to melatonin, the hormone which promotes sleep.
- **Stay hydrated.** Good hydration begins when you wake up in the morning, before you even go to the toilet. Hydrating all day long is important for your bowels, your skin, and so you don't confuse hunger for thirst. It also keeps you energised during the day, and helps you sleep well at night. However, try not to drink too much after 6 pm so a full bladder won't disturb your sleep.

Can you catch up on sleep?

Can getting extra sleep on the weekend help you catch up on what you missed during the week? Perhaps. In a study of over 2000 participants, those who slept longer on the weekend had a lower body mass index (BMI) than those who didn't. In addition, it appears that the BMI relationship was dose dependent – that is, every extra hour of weekend sleep was associated with lower body mass. So it's possible that you can catch up on sleep and still maintain a healthy weight.

However I think creating good sleep habits is really important – and is probably the easiest routine to stick to, in the long term. In my clinical practice, I see better results with consistent sleep rather than 'banked' sleep.

CASE STUDY
The worn-out medico

Janet Spruce, 57, doctor

'When my sister told me I had middle-aged spread, I didn't know what to say. I'd always been the 'thin' sister – compared to her, at least! But when I turned 50 and hit menopause, it was true: I put on weight, seven kilos in a year.

I blamed the weight on hormone replacement therapy, but there was more going on than that. I wasn't sleeping well, which is a symptom of menopause. Because I was tired, I wasn't exercising, and then I was eating to compensate for my fatigue. As you can imagine, none of this helped my waistline, or my energy levels. And I really can't afford to have a drop in energy: I'm a doctor with three teenage kids. I've got stuff to do!

Once I started to see Michele, prepping meals became part of my weekends and was a key micro habit in my life. I also started to practise yoga and meditate regularly, which I think helped reduce my cortisol, which then helped me lose weight. You'd think, as a doctor, I'd have had the answers to all of this, but I didn't. Thank goodness for Michele!'

My non-negotiable #2

EXERCISE

What if there were a magic pill that could help with your depression, weight, posture, energy and sleep, with no negative side effects. Would you consider it?

You would? Amazing. Because it exists. It's called exercise, and it's about as close to a magic bullet for health as you'll ever get.

Exercise can seem daunting to many of us because we think of it as painful, time consuming or unrewarding. But it doesn't have to be, if you choose a form of exercise you like – and trust me, there is something out there for everyone. You don't have to spend hours and hours exercising each day

to benefit, either. But you do have to exercise. It's a non-negotiable.

Again, do not compromise. Make time to exercise, and do whatever you can to get your exercise scheduled in and done. Don't make excuses to other people about not doing it, and definitely don't make excuses to yourself!

Micro habits for regular exercise

Seek out a HIIT (high-intensity interval training) class once or twice a week. Don't be put off by the name: HIIT is simply about doing 60–90 seconds of exercise at full capacity to increase your heart rate, followed by about 30 seconds of rest. Some studies show that just 20 minutes of this type of exercise each day can be effective for weight loss. Your local gym will probably have HIIT classes, and there are plenty of HIIT apps you can download to work out with at home.

Train with weights. Weight training is not about becoming a bodybuilder. On the contrary, all I want you to do is incorporate some sort of resistance training – like lifting weights, or using your own body weight to perform push-ups and squats – a few times a week. Weight training builds muscle, and muscle burns more calories than fat – up to three times more, in fact. In short, muscles are fat-burning machines, and the more muscle you have, the more calories you'll burn. Weight training also prolongs your calorie burn – once your exercise session has finished, your body will still be burning energy for the next 24–48 hours!

Stretch yourself – literally and figuratively. If you think Pilates, yoga and stretching are a waste of time, think again. I also used to think the only exercise worth doing was heart-pumping cardio, but then I found a yoga class that felt like a massage and a lovely big stretch, all in one, and I was hooked. These classes help you maintain flexibility, strength and posture – all keys to growing old gracefully. Find a class that works for you, and stick with it.

Remember that the best exercise is the one you will do. Jogging, cycling, circuit classes, Pilates, Barre, boxing, even just brisk walking – find what you like doing, and do it. If you're really struggling, rope in a buddy. Exercising with a friend makes you more accountable and more likely to stick with it. You'll both be better off.

'Remember that the best exercise is the one you will do.'

My non-negotiable #3

FIND WAYS TO BUST STRESS

When it comes to belly fat, most of us think those extra servings of hot chips are to blame. Of course, such foods are not completely innocent, but the factors involved in weight gain are more complicated than that.

Cortisol, our stress hormone, is a belly-fat culprit we rarely think of, but it's hugely important.

The simple act of constant stress – physical, mental or even imaginary stress – makes our adrenals pump cortisol, which in turn, pumps glucose. Hello, adrenal fatigue and belly fat.

When we have too much glucose in our bodies, our insulin receptors essentially get tired and stop working; we can become insulin-resistant. When this happens, we become one of those people who just look at food and seem to gain weight.

If you feel like you're eating well but seem to be weight-loss resistant, this should be a big red alert. Are you just a 'stress head' creating insulin havoc?

A fear of
the
unknown?

Your job?

Your
family?

What type of stress is
hacking your waistline?

Your
finances?

Chaotic
thoughts?

Your partner?

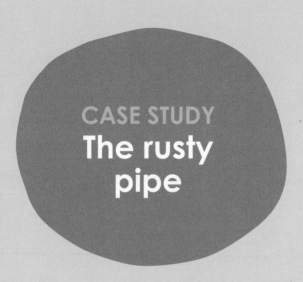

The rusty pipe

Janise Sammons, 62, retired

'Before I started seeing Michele, I was the classic skinny, bloated, dehydrated rusty pipe. I wasn't overweight, but at 65 kilos, with most of it on my belly, I looked like I was having a 'change of life' baby – at 59!

It was a phone call from my friend Kaye while I was on holiday (drinking champagne!) that changed the course of my life. Kaye asked if I was interested in joining her for a Cleanse and Nourish program. I cut my holiday short, left my bewildered husband and returned home to get healthy.

There was no gentle easing in: Michele told me immediately what I needed to do. Quit the coffee, alcohol, gluten, salty crackers, cheese, sugar, lolly snakes and chips. It was tough. Really tough. But I stuck to it, because I knew I needed to do something for my health.

The first week was challenging, but by the second week, I'd dropped four kilos. Four weeks in, I was down to 59 kilos, but even better, I was clear-eyed, clear-headed and full of beans.

Five years later, I still do the cleanse every February to kick off the new year the right way. Every year, I learn new things and new Michele-isms. (My favourite is, "Your medicine is at the end of your fork.") The rest of the year, I eat well, but I indulge in great food and wine when I want to. Michele taught me that I can eat out, I just need some rules. I order greens as much as possible, avoid gluten (except if I'm in France and the pastries are not to be missed), drink plenty of water and embrace intermittent fasting to get back on the wagon.

Michele taught me that I can live life and still maintain a healthy weight. I haven't looked back.'

Micro habits to manage stress

- Practise meditation and mindfulness. This doesn't mean sitting cross-legged on a pillow, holding beads as you hum and inhale the scent of patchouli – though it can, if that's your jam. Meditation can be done anywhere, anytime. In your work clothes taking a much-needed breather, in your car while you're waiting for your children, in a park, on a bench, sitting at your kitchen table. (I've been known to sneak into conference rooms!) Meditation is simply about letting your mind be quiet. This lowers your heart rate, calms your galloping thoughts and allows you to be present and mindful. And when we are present, mindful and calm, our cortisol stops racing through our veins.

- Try yoga nidra. Right now, if you haven't heard of it already, I want you to stop what you're doing and Google 'yoga nidra'. Take 10 or 20 minutes to listen to one of the sessions you find, and then come back. How do you feel? Yoga nidra, or yogic sleep, is a deep state of relaxation – it's basically somewhere between sleeping and waking. You don't have to be in a dark room wearing a tie-dyed shirt with incense burning, but try to find a quiet, calm place to lie down. Your body becomes completely relaxed as a voice guides you into slowly relaxing different parts of your body. For those with busy minds, it's awesome – your mind follows the guided talk, allowing your body to deeply relax. Try it, please, and see how you feel.

- Relax mindfully. I'm wary of using the word 'mindful', as we often get caught up in the definition, thinking of mindfulness as something we need to do at a certain time, so that mindfulness, ironically, can sound like a lot of work! But mindfulness is all about getting us back to calmness, or having one thought process at a time. Doesn't that sound nice? One task at a time, so that we can complete it purposefully, with a clear head. So, create a micro habit, every day, to do one thing mindfully – whether it's walking your dog for 15 minutes, or gardening for half an hour. No phones, no chatter, just the task at hand. Try starting your mindful activity with a simple breathing exercise: slowly inhale through your nose for a count of four, hold your breath for a count of seven, and then exhale through your mouth for a count of eight. Do four rounds. In the beginning, do it to quick counts, then lengthen as it becomes a habit. Once you feel the effects of calm breathing, it will become a habit, because you'll love the immediate relaxing effect on your heart, breath and mind. I know I do.

MY STORY:

The reluctant meditator

My own experience with meditation has been... interesting. About 15 years ago, I rocked up to a meditation class at my friend Libby's home. At the time, I had three babies, a husband who was constantly on the road for work and a head full of monkey chatter. My life was crazy busy. I was desperate for calm that didn't come in the form of one too many wines, as I knew deep down that this only left me exhausted, fuzzy and bloated the next day.

So I went along to Libby's. Our teacher was a lovely woman named Amara. She was the real deal – I'm talking hemp pants, a necklace of mala beads, patchouli oil as perfume, a face free of make-up.

As much as I wanted to have her sense of calm, my type A personality just wouldn't allow it. I couldn't stand the class. After eight sessions, I told Amara that I had another commitment and would not be coming back. She nodded and took my hands. Very quietly, she said, 'Michele, you are welcome to come back whenever your good heart is ready. Please know this: creating a life that goes at a modest, calm pace is not about being slow, inefficient or mediocre. In fact, it will manifest the exact opposite.'

Boom. You know how Oprah talks about 'a-ha' moments? Well, that was one of mine.

A few months later, I resumed my classes with Amara, and to this day, I do yoga with her every week. I was initially sceptical about yoga's ability to help me find clarity and stillness within a calm, peaceful mind and body – but please, give it a go, and you will find it takes your creativity, clarity and kindness to another level. Take this micro habit slow, and keep exploring until it feels right for you. A great way to begin is to try an app like Calm or Headspace.

My non-negotiable #4

PRACTISE GRATITUDE

The simple notion of gratitude can seem a little contrived, old-fashioned or 'self-helpy'. But, actually, there's a lot of research on the benefits of expressing gratitude. When you start to practise gratitude every day, you will feel your mood lifting, and the flow-on wellness effects this brings. So quash your inner cynic and give it a go.

Numerous studies over many years have found that the act of expressing gratitude leads to greater happiness and fewer incidences of depression. While the field of psychology is often about 'fixing', this model of positive psychology is about amplifying wellness. Think of it as preventive health for your mind.

I firmly believe that gratitude can also benefit our physical health. In our busy world,

I'm constantly looking for solutions that are not too taxing for my clients, yet yield great results. Since it's scientifically proven that people who are happier and less depressed are better able to nourish themselves with food, sleep and exercise, and since we know that happy people practise gratitude regularly, I want you to develop a gratitude micro habit.

Micro habits for gratitude

Write in a journal. Every day, write down three things you are grateful for and why. You can keep an old-fashioned journal, or simply write them in the Notes app on your phone. Keep the points specific. I like to do this in the middle of a busy day when I'm eating lunch: it gives me pause, and because I'm thinking happy thoughts, my cortisol is naturally lowered. Honestly, it can be as simple as this. Here are my three things from the other day.

- I am so appreciative of my husband, Steven, bringing me tea to the bathroom this morning when I was getting ready, without me asking. He knew I would love it, but he also knew I didn't want to ask because I wouldn't want to seem like a bossy boots!
- I am grateful that my hair is growing back. I lost a lot of hair when my brother, Greg, died. I always took my hair for granted, until it became super thin and I realised how much I like the thick, frizzy hair I had. Now that it's growing back, I am grateful for every little strand.
- I'm thankful for my friend Libby. She is such a wonderful supporter of, and advocate for, women working to find their purpose. When you're working hard in your own business, you can often feel outside the friendship loop. Libby always takes the time to hook me in and make me feel welcome.

Write a thank-you note. Everyone loves thank-you notes. It doesn't matter if it's a text, email or the super-nice touch of a handwritten note. People love to be acknowledged and appreciated. And sending out your thank-you notes will make you feel good, too. It's a win–win.

The comfort eater

Danielle Martin, 34, nurse

'I was always the heavy girl. During high school and university, my weight yo-yoed constantly. After having my second child, I was ready for a solution – not a quick fix. I wanted to put the years of fluctuation behind me and finally get healthy.

Being Italian and a lover of great food, I was apprehensive about any program that restricted food. But Michele showed me that by eating smart carbs, fats and protein, I could eat the most incredible food and never feel hungry. Now, I don't turn to junk food for comfort; there is more in my life. I still get pleasure from food – but I never rely on it to make me feel good.

I drink occasionally, but I don't need a drink to help me relax. Now I do yoga and meditation, and those things help me much more than a glass of wine or a beer ever did.

The biggest mind shift for me was realising that I am on my own journey; it's no use comparing myself to others. After all, we all have different goals and achieve them at different times.

The best thing you can do for yourself is stay in your own lane while cheering everyone else on. And trust that these small changes can lead to huge amounts of happiness.'

My non-negotiable #5

BANISH GUILT

As adults, one of our superpowers is feeling guilty over small things, and endlessly berating ourselves. This self-sabotage needs to stop, right now.

I want you to make a commitment to stop beating yourself up for a poor dinner choice or having one too many wines. Acknowledge that you did, and move on. Because here's the thing: you cannot fail at good nutrition. Don't starve yourself the morning after a binge to 'correct' your behaviour. All you need to do is pick up where you left off.

If you're a bit of a weekend warrior – a wine or two on Friday night with some chips, or half a pepperoni pizza with the family on Saturday – then acknowledge it and consciously decide, without guilt, when you're going to indulge, and when you're going to get back to abundant, nourishing foods.

Make a plan, stick to it, and when you do indulge, make it a mindful choice, enjoy it and stop feeling guilty.

I would like you to take the #noguilt thing one step further. You may not feel able to take time out for nourishing activities such as exercise, meditation or having a massage. You might see these things as 'luxuries', but I assure you they are not. When you feel the benefits of true wellness – mentally, physically and emotionally – you become more productive, open-hearted and creative.

I have witnessed this on many occasions with clients. Seeing people be nicer to themselves – and the knock-on effect this has on their lives and relationships – is nothing short of astounding. Many times it has brought me to tears; it's a wonderful reminder that the best thing we can do for ourselves is to support ourselves as best we can. It begins with simple acts like this.

Micro habits for #noguilt

- **Create a conscious plan for a reckless night.** This may sound odd, but visualise in your mind what a night out or party night might entail for you. Nachos, chicken wings and a few margaritas? Burgers, chips and a few beers? Now that you have that image in your mind's eye, write a plan down (here and on your phone) on how you will move on from the guilt the next day. That plan needs to include eating, and not deprivation. So if your Friday night was a bit of a binge, then Saturday morning might include poached eggs with lots of veggies followed by a walk. It is when we say 'I am not eating because I have a food baby from last night' mode that our guilt makes us spiral into yet another binge.

- **Plan, schedule and pay for a regular indulgence.** Healthy indulgences are not luxuries, they are necessities if we want to start being kinder to our mind and body. There is a knock-on effect of planning things like massages, hikes, mini trips, facials, yoga weekends, a day of fishing, boating or a simple picnic. When we allow ourselves these joys without guilt, we mentally feel better. When our head is in a good space, we are less likely to emotionally beat ourselves up with poor food choices.

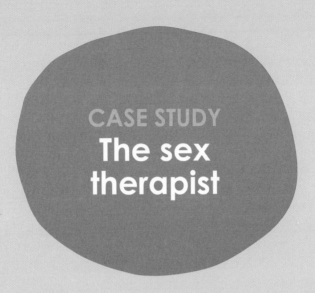

CASE STUDY
The sex therapist

Dr Nikki Goldstein, 32, sexologist

'Four years ago, I was exhausted, unhealthy – and confused. I've always struggled with my weight, trying various fad diets to try to stick to a food plan that worked for me. It probably won't surprise you to hear that restricting food groups didn't work! It was only when I met Michele that I began to realise that, actually, eating healthily is not as scary – or difficult – as I'd imagined.

Michele taught me that I could have a glass of wine or piece of chocolate, so long as it was a balanced part of my life. She taught me that these things weren't 'naughty', but rather, indulgences to look forward to and savour.

One of the best things about working with Michele has been the discussions we've had about body image. Our focus has been health and weight loss, but one of the positive side effects has been that the attention has actually been taken away from how I look. Now, it's not the number on the scales that matters so much, but how I'm feeling. Today, I would rather be heavier but be healthy and have energy and feel vibrant. It took a long time to get my head around that. I think that as women, we are just taught to look at the numbers on the scales.

Today, I feel sexier in my body because I feel healthy. It's not even so much about how I look on the outside, it's more my own mindset. No one wants to have sex when they feel bloated and tired! My confidence soared, too, when I began feeling healthier, and my relationships improved. I mean, people like being around happy people!'

You absolutely can maintain your wellbeing and your waistline when dining out or on holiday. The majority of my clients are busy people, working hard but also dining out often for work or pleasure.

Don't be afraid. Once you begin to trust that you have cemented your micro habits, you can trust the process of 'Eat, Drink & Still Shrink'.

Eating out without blowing out

I'm inclined to agree with nearly everything the legendary American chef Julia Child ever said, and her famous adage that 'People who love to eat are the best people' is something I turn back to again and again – because I find it's so true!

For me, one of life's pleasures is going to a restaurant or café and indulging in delicious food and wine. The good news is, I give you full permission to do this. I promise you won't blow out your health goals – if you follow a few key points.

- Don't fill up on bread. Unless we're talking about bread from an award-winning bakery, with flour hand-milled by angels, I don't see the point in wasting calories on bread. Personally, I'd rather enjoy a glass of pinot.
- P, F and CC. When ordering, seek out your P, F and CC – protein, healthy fats and complex carbs. You'll find you can follow this simple rule pretty much everywhere. At Thai restaurants, for example, you might choose a curry with an extra serve of vegetables and no rice, or brown rice instead of white. At an Italian restaurant, go for veal escalope with vegetables.
- Choose your poison, and be okay with it. Eating out is a treat, and you are allowed to treat yourself. If you really want a bowl of pasta, eat it, enjoy it – and then move on. Don't feel guilty about it!
- Consider not having dessert. Personally, I'd rather fill my plate with a herbed salmon fillet, or a juicy grass-fed beef fillet, not a ton of sugar. If you love dessert, please go ahead and enjoy it – but if you only have it out of habit, consider why you're doing this. Maybe a short black or cup of tea would be a sweeter way to finish.
- Crowd it out. Ask for an extra serve of vegetables. Don't be afraid to ask for salad or vegetables instead of chips or potatoes. You're the customer! It's up to you.

Eat, drink & still shrink on holidays

Just as I love eating out, I also love travelling. And when I go away, I like to indulge and eat local foods and let my hair down a bit. But, as with eating out, I follow a few guidelines to ensure I don't bring back five extra kilos as a souvenir.

- Beware the buffet. Just because it's called 'all you can eat', this doesn't mean you have to eat it all. When filling your plate, think about whether the foods you've chosen are going to make you feel nourished and ready for a day of sightseeing, or whether they're going to make you feel heavy and bloated.

- Careful with cocktails. Look, I get it: cocktails look and taste good. And when you're on holiday, it's fun to sit in a beach chair sipping a margarita. But one too many could leave you with a heavy sugar bloat. Some cocktails have up to 25 teaspoons of sugar in just one serve. One serve! Isn't that crazy? Again, choose your poison. Refer to the list of cocktails on page 133 for better, lower-sugar options.

Holiday weight-loss syndrome

While for many of us, going on holiday can lead to weight gain, for some people it actually helps them lose weight. I know, it sounds a bit mad, but has this ever happened to you? Have you left for your holiday chubbier than usual? Did you have grand plans to lose a few kilos before you left to fit into that new bikini, but instead you were flat-out at work and actually ended up gaining weight in the lead-up?

But then something funny happens. You have a ball on your holiday. You eat, you have a few glasses of champagne, you swim and walk and generally have a great time. You forget about those pesky kilos.

You get back, expecting to be a lot bigger than when you left. But there you are, looking lean and energised. You've had a fabulous holiday because you didn't beat yourself up. You ate well, laughed a lot and even drank more wine than usual. You were not in your usual state of busyness, and yet you lost a couple of kilos without even thinking about it.

So what changed? Busy-itis. You were not setting your alarm, rushing for your coffee, barrelling into a spin class all before 7 am so you could get home to say goodbye to the kids before you set off for the office for a 9 am meeting. Or maybe you're not physically stressed out, but when you're at home, you feel mentally stressed because you can't control the monkey chatter in your head.

How on earth does this happen?

As we saw earlier, when we are in a constant state of stress, our adrenal glands are turned on for longer than we actually need. Adrenal glands are wonderful powerhouses that give us cortisol, which gets our glucose pumping. The glucose is delivered to the cells and, provided that the cells' insulin receptors are open and ready, the glucose goes in and is used for energy. Think of this receptor like a slide, sliding glucose into our cells. Our bodies are wonderful until we push them over the edge and damage this slide. If our cells are constantly getting glucose from adrenal stress and cortisol overload, the insulin receptors get annoyed and begin to close up, leaving glucose outside the cell, creating blood sugar and insulin chaos. This chaos just ends up making us chubby, tired and bloated.

But we can break the cycle by finding ways to deal with stress. Take more time out to do the things you really enjoy, or create new micro habits to support your physical and mental wellbeing.

4

Preparing for the plan

Now that we know what our micro habits are, what our ideal day looks like and the habits we're trying to break, it's time to put our plan into action. And, like all good plans, ours starts with breakfast. Most of us don't have time in the mornings to fuss around with complicated recipes, so keep your breakfast simple and quick.

EGGS FOR BREAKFAST

Three of my favourite ways to serve eggs

**Poached eggs
on wilted spinach
with lemon, avocado
and mushrooms**

Scrambled eggs, with roast veggies from the night before mixed through

Hard-boiled eggs on a bed of rocket with hummus

Eggs are one of our best protein choices. Full of amino acids and vitamins that assist with our skin, hair, nails, brain function and more, they're also inexpensive and readily available. And don't worry about the idea that eggs will give you high cholesterol or heart issues; the cholesterol in eggs has almost no effect on your blood cholesterol levels.

The magic combo

As with all meals, breakfast needs to be a combination of protein, quality fats and smart carbs. As long as you have a mix of these three macronutrients, you can't go wrong. And of course, you can always add a pinch of spice or a little something to make your tastebuds come alive. Think of how tasty eggs with salsa, guacamole or pesto can be.

TOAST FOR BREAKFAST

Three delicious ways with toast

Grainy toast with
olive oil, sliced
tomato and chopped
hard-boiled egg

Sweet potato 'toast'
with avocado, smoked
salmon and capers

Gluten-free charcoal
toast with pesto and
goat's cheese

Choose a good-quality spelt, rye, grain or gluten-free bread (such as buckwheat, brown rice or charcoal bread), and add your toppings. You could even slice a sweet potato slightly thinner than a bread slice, and toast it or warm it in a sandwich press – trust me, it's delicious.

OATS FOR BREAKFAST

Three sweet ideas for breakfast

Berry yoghurt bowl with toasted nuts and seeds, shredded coconut and a pinch of cinnamon

Oats cooked with a teaspoon of coconut oil, topped with mixed seeds or nuts, cinnamon and cacao nibs

Oats with plain full-fat Greek-style yoghurt, vanilla bean paste, 1 teaspoon pea protein powder mix and berries

For a sweet breakfast that still delivers all your nutritional needs, choose a bowl of nourishing oats or yoghurt. Oats provide slow-release energy to keep you feeling fuller for longer, and yoghurt is a wonderful source of protein and calcium.

DINNER FOR LUNCH

Turn dinner recipes into lunch-friendly meals.

Meatball salad bowl

Take the turkey meatballs from page 154 and transform them into a salad bowl by adding cooked brown rice and fresh greens, and seasoning with olive oil, salt and pepper. Sprinkle some flaxseeds on top and you're ready to go!

Tahini chicken salad

Make a salad with the roast chicken
and cauli from page 190 – just add
a green leaf of your choice, ¼ tin
drained chickpeas, some diced
red capsicum and thinly sliced
red onion, then drizzle over the
tahini sauce as a dressing.

Fishcake salad

Serve the fishcakes from page
166 with a rocket, tomato and
cucumber salad dressed with olive
oil and your favourite vinegar.

In my experience, lunch is often an afterthought – something we grab when we remember we need to eat. Eating a proper lunch, replete with protein, smart carbs and healthy fat, will help us work productively, with heaps of energy, all through the afternoon and save us becoming insanely hungry and cranky at 4 pm! I love making extra batches of dinner and turning them into lunches later in the week – a cheap, efficient and easy way to nourish yourself.

Where's the bread?

While having the occasional sandwich or wrap (on good-quality grainy or dark bread) is fine, sandwiches are often very high in carbs and low in protein. Once a week is okay, but don't eat them more often than this. And please, don't use white bread! It has the nutritional properties of playdough. After all, it's made of the same ingredients: flour, water and salt.

PROTEIN
chicken breast
eggs
tuna
salmon

FATS
feta
avocado
full-fat Greek-style yoghurt
hummus
nuts

CARBS
quinoa
brown rice
rye bread
chickpeas

MIX & MATCH LUNCH

There are endless combos
so you'll never get bored!

Another easy way to build a nutritious lunch is the mix and match approach. Choose your favourite combinations of protein, healthy fats and smart carbs, then pile on some greens and crunchy veg and serve. You can pre-cook your proteins and grains in batches beforehand to make lunchtimes even easier.

My favourite combos

1. 1 x 185 g tin tuna, ¼ cup cooked brown rice and 1 cup baby spinach (this may seem a lot, but you'll be happy when you are not searching for something sweet in an hour!)
2. Two boiled eggs, half an avocado and a slice of rye bread.
3. ¼ cup quinoa, cherry tomatoes and 200 g roast chicken breast (supermarkets now sell cooked organic chicken, making this a really easy option for a last-minute lunch).

DINNER

Because dinner is the meal we're most likely to cook regularly at home, I've created 28 simple, tasty and healthy dinners for you, starting on page 145. As with anything in life, if a meal is simple to prepare, you'll make it again and again.

Each recipe is packed with quality protein, fats and primarily non-starchy vegetables. (We don't need starchy vegetables at night as much, as our energy requirements are winding down.) Your evening meal should be as light as possible, and once you get into this habit, it becomes second nature.

How to use these recipes

You'll see that I've sometimes included variations on a recipe. Sometimes these are to provide extra energy, so other family members (a young child, teenager or active spouse) can also enjoy the meal. When you make these meals with starchy vegetables or smart carbs, always make extra for your breakfast or lunch the next day.

To keep your life simple, whenever you can double the recipe when cooking dinner, to use as the basis of your lunch the following day. Believe me, this will be tastier than takeaway options, far cheaper and definitely healthier!

My key micro habit: the one-night fast

Once a week, I want you to skip dinner and do what I call 'micro fasting'. This is an easy form of intermittent fasting that will have a big impact on your waistline.

Intermittent fasting comes in many forms (the 5:2 Diet, 16:8, etc), and entails giving our bodies a break from food so that we can use up excess glucose and improve our insulin sensitivity.

Insulin is our fat storage hormone, and when it's sluggish or becoming resistant, we gain weight easily, even if we eat like birds! We want our insulin receptors to be awake and functioning, and one effective way to do this is with intermittent fasting. (HIIT and weight training also help, too.)

While there's a lot of information out there about fasting, the simplest way to do it is to avoid dinner – and other evening foods – once a week. Yep – that's all I want you to do. Throughout the day, eat normally, as we've talked about already, and then stop eating at 4 pm. After that you can have a cup of herbal tea or some broth, but nothing else until you wake up the next day.

Some people like to reverse this and skip breakfast, but I've found that intermittent fasting at night is far more effective for weight loss.

Before you start, here are some practical tips.

- Don't fast more than once a week, otherwise you'll find you experience a 'rebound effect' and get even hungrier than usual.
- Fast on a night when you can rest and get into bed early.
- Don't restrict calories at other times. I don't want you to starve, obsess about not eating, have hunger pangs or suffer brain fog, because these will set you off on a binge eventually.
- If you're a parent, don't do this at the dinner table with your family. Choose another evening when you might be out for work or at a school meeting, or switch to morning fasting instead. We want to encourage a love of food in front of our children, not fear.

Spice it up

Need a little spice in your life? Who doesn't? To add some flair to your cooking, spice up your meals – all of them! Invest in good-quality spice mixes to have on hand to add to meals, dressings or sides.

A pinch of Mexican seasoning is amazing with smashed avocado. Chilli and garlic salt mixed into your oil and lemon dressing gives your salad or roast vegetables a delicious boost. Cinnamon in porridge, a little cayenne pepper or paprika on boiled eggs – you get the picture. Spices make meals exciting, so don't be afraid to use them. You can find a host of amazing spices, free of additives and preservatives, in your local supermarket these days.

Your flavour cheat sheet

Take your tastebuds on a joyride through the great cuisines
of the world with these classic flavour combinations.

Italian
Basil, oregano, parsley,
rosemary, garlic

Mexican
Coriander, paprika, cumin, chilli,
oregano, garlic, cinnamon

Thai
Ginger, coriander, lemongrass,
garlic, Thai basil, chilli, mint

Chinese
Garlic, cloves, black pepper,
cinnamon, fennel, chilli

Moroccan
Paprika, cumin, ginger,
saffron, turmeric

Indian
Ginger, turmeric, coriander, cumin,
bay leaves, cardamom, nutmeg, mustard
seeds, garlic, garam masala, cinnamon,
chilli, curry powder

Swap this for that

Creating micro habits is all about making small adjustments over time to help ensure you're living your healthiest life. When it comes to great food choices, here are some small tweaks you can make that, over time, will add up to big results for you.

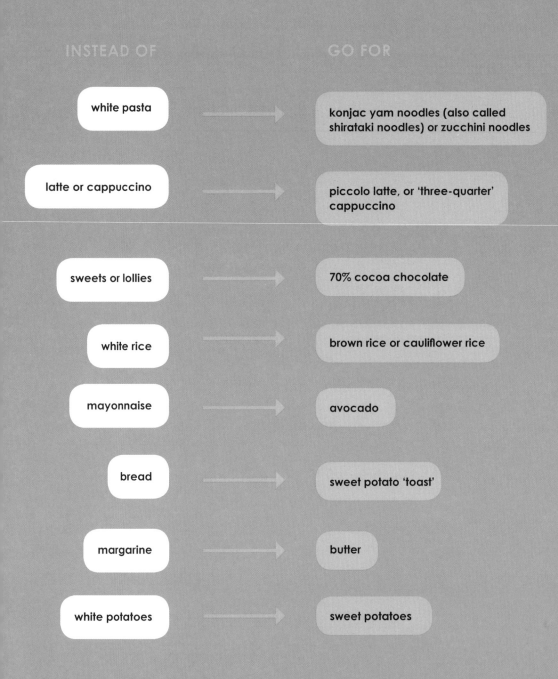

INSTEAD OF	GO FOR
white pasta	konjac yam noodles (also called shirataki noodles) or zucchini noodles
latte or cappuccino	piccolo latte, or 'three-quarter' cappuccino
sweets or lollies	70% cocoa chocolate
white rice	brown rice or cauliflower rice
mayonnaise	avocado
bread	sweet potato 'toast'
margarine	butter
white potatoes	sweet potatoes

soft drinks	→	soda water spiked with fresh lemon or lime
ketchup or tomato sauce	→	salsa, hummus, pesto or mustard
cocktails	→	white spirits (like gin or vodka) with soda and fresh lemon or lime juice
bread with your dinner	→	an extra side of vegetables
muffins	→	protein-packed smoothies
sweet wine like moscato	→	champagne or dry prosecco
muesli bar	→	fresh fruit or a small portion of nuts
sweetened yoghurts	→	plain full-fat Greek-style yoghurt
sweet biscuits	→	brown rice crackers or seed and grain crackers with almond butter
white flour	→	almond flour
vegetable oils like canola, corn and soybean	→	cold-pressed extra virgin olive oil, butter, ghee, coconut oil, avocado oil and walnut oil

Life's little pleasures: coffee & alcohol

You work hard. Life is short. So, let's do the best we can with food and exercise – but, honestly, there's no need to live without coffee or alcohol, unless of course you are pregnant, or abstain from these drinks due to religious or medical reasons.

Coffee

First up, coffee is not bad for us. Sure, too much coffee is bad for us, just as too much of anything is bad for us. But in a recent study with data from over half a million people, the author concluded that coffee is absolutely fine in moderation, noting that these results provide further evidence that coffee drinking can be part of a healthy diet.

However, please be aware that coffee is not a good energy source. If you're tired at 3 pm, you need to ask yourself if you slept well the night before. If you didn't, then you need to prioritise sleep, not an extra piccolo. If sleep isn't the issue, have you fed yourself well enough?

In short, coffee should be consumed because it is enjoyable, rather than being relied on to get you through your busy day. Good food, with quality fats, protein and smart carbs, are what will really let you power on all day.

Dos and don'ts

DON'T: Load your coffee with sugary or artificial sweeteners.

DON'T: Drink more than two coffees per day.

DO: Drink all your coffee before midday, to minimise any impact on quality sleep.

DO: Drink organic coffee, or as close to organic as you can. Coffee crops are known for their pesticide use, and we just don't know enough about their effects yet.

DON'T: Drink decaffeinated. Coffee is heavily processed to become decaffeinated. Why not simply move to a strong, bitter herbal tea (like dandelion) for the same punch, or make the switch completely and become a herbal tea drinker? This might be a new micro habit for you.

Wine, beer and alcohol

Pinot and piccolos are my partners in crime (yours might be cab sav and cappuccinos), but I don't abuse them or I suffer the consequences. With even one glass of wine too many, I feel sluggish and fuzzy the next day, not to mention puffy – especially in the face!

In moderation, however, there's nothing wrong with a glass of wine. Look at the Mediterranean diet, widely regarded as one of the healthiest in the world, where a glass of wine is customary with many meals. Personally, during the working week, I like to enjoy two drinks a night (maximum!), with at least two alcohol-free nights a week. It's a nice indulgence and a lovely way to unwind.

Dos and don'ts

DON'T: Binge. Look, we all have the occasional binge on the weekend, but we suffer from it, overeat the next day and generally feel like crap. If you do binge regularly, ask yourself why that is.

DO: Be aware just how much sugar your favourite beverage contains. Many cocktails (see opposite) have a surprising amount of added sugar, so avoid these and opt for a low-sugar beverage, like vodka and soda water with lemon, lime, mint, lemongrass or something else to add flavour. If you like tonic water, try 'sonic' – half soda, half tonic. (Soda water has no added sugar, whereas tonic water does.) Eventually, you might be able to shift to being a soda drinker.

DO: Choose your poison. Champagne and wine, believe it or not, are not packed with sugar. Sure, they have a little sugar, but nowhere near as much as soft drink, for instance, so they're both good options if you'd like to enjoy a drink. Beer, though, is often higher in calories than wine and spirits, so if you find you are getting a bit of a beer belly, make the switch to wine or a spirit like gin or vodka (it's often the gluten and/or yeast in beer that causes the bloat).

Sugar! Is that what's in my drink?

When it comes to hidden sugar, cocktails can sure pack a punch. Here's how much sugar is in your favourite cocktails according to myfitnesspal.com.

Piña Colada, 425 ml glass:
63 g (15.75 teaspoons) sugar

Sex on the Beach, 425 ml glass:
48 g (12 teaspoons) sugar

Long Island Iced Tea, 400 ml glass:
40 g (10 teaspoons) sugar

Pimm's, 400 ml glass:
32 g (8 teaspoons) sugar

Whiskey Sour, 220ml glass:
29 g (7.5 teaspoons) sugar

Mojito, 225 ml glass:
25 g (6.25 teaspoons) sugar

BETTER LOW-SUGAR OPTIONS

Gin & Sonic: **less than 8 g
(2 teaspoons) sugar**
30 ml gin with half soda water
and half tonic water, served with
a slice of cucumber

Margarita (WITHOUT
premade mix): **less than 8 g,
(2 teaspoons) sugar**
30 ml tequila, fresh lime juice
and a splash of agave syrup

Moscow Mule: **less than 8 g,
or 2 teaspoons sugar**
30 ml vodka, soda, lots of mint
leaves and lime juice and a
splash of ginger beer

Wine or champagne,
150 ml : **about
2 g sugar**

Martini: **less than 1 g sugar**
50 ml gin or vodka,
10 ml dry vermouth, 3 green
olives and splash of olive brine

SMART SHOPPING

I'm a big believer in surrounding yourself with the things you need to achieve success. So here's what I fill my fridge, pantry and fruit bowl with, to ensure I always eat well.

Fresh fruit & veg

FRUIT

These are low in sugar and can be enjoyed daily.

- Apples
- Berries – strawberries, blueberries, raspberries
- Grapefruit
- Kiwifruit
- Lemons and limes for teas and water
- Pears

STARCHY VEGETABLES

Limit starchy vegetables to once or twice a day, preferably at breakfast or lunch. This is so we can use that 'smart carb' as fuel for our brain and energy.

- Artichokes
- Beetroot
- Carrots
- Celeriac
- Corn
- Edamame beans
- Parsnips
- Potatoes
- Pumpkin
- Sweet potatoes
- Yams

NON-STARCHY & LOW-STARCH VEGETABLES

- Asparagus
- Avocado
- Bok choy
- Broccoli*
- Brussels sprouts*
- Cabbage*
- Capsicum
- Cauliflower*
- Celery
- Cucumber
- Dandelion greens
- Eggplant
- Fennel
- Green beans
- Green lettuces
- Kale*
- Konjac noodles (made from the Japanese konjac yam, and also known as shirataki noodles – your new pasta!)
- Leeks
- Mushrooms (all mushrooms are okay, but shiitake are the best!)
- Olives
- Onion
- Peas
- Pickled or fermented vegetables
- Radish
- Rocket
- Spinach
- Sprouts (both bean sprouts and alfalfa sprouts)
- Tomatoes
- Turnips
- Watercress
- Zucchini

* Brassica vegetables are some of my favourites! They are excellent at cleansing the liver and I recommend including them in your meals at least once a day. If your thyroid is sluggish, eat them cooked rather than raw. These vegetables contain goitrogens, which can affect your thyroid by enlarging your thyroid gland or slowing it down. But by slightly cooking brassicas, you change their molecular structure, thus removing this goitrogenic effect.

In the fridge & pantry

GOOD FATS

Remember, quality fats don't make you fat. Fats are satiating, making you less likely to crave sugar, junk or high-carb foods.

- Coconut milk (and kefir)
- Coconut oil
- Cold-pressed extra virgin olive oil
- Extra virgin flaxseed oil
- Extra virgin nut oils – hazelnut, macadamia and walnut
- Ghee
- Unrefined toasted sesame oil

I usually use an inexpensive extra virgin olive oil for general cooking, and a good-quality extra virgin olive oil or a nut oil for dressings and drizzling over cooked food. Extra virgin olive oil has three key qualities that make it an excellent choice to cook with: it is a stable fat, it has low levels of fatty acids and high levels of protective antioxidants. When cooking Asian meals, I like to use coconut oil or ghee, and a splash of sesame oil to round out the dish.

GRAINS

There is a 'grain phobia' happening and it needs to stop. Sure, some people will not digest grains without tummy discomfort, but for most of us they are a great source of vitamin B. The grains listed below are high in 'smart carbs' and have a bit of protein as well. I have seen how consuming a small amount of grains at breakfast and lunch can really help a person's adrenal fatigue.

Gluten free

- Basmati rice
- Brown rice – my favourite as it's so nutritious
- Brown rice cakes
- Buckwheat (note: this is not a type of wheat!)
- Gluten-free bread – buckwheat is best
- Millet
- Quinoa

Non gluten-free

- Couscous (wholewheat, if possible)
- Freekeh
- Oats – 'rolled' or 'steel cut', but not instant

PROTEIN

In a perfect world, it would be wonderful to consume grass-fed, organic proteins all the time. We don't live in a perfect world, so just do the best you can.

- Milk: I like A2 milk because it's less likely to cause digestive issues or, if you prefer, non-dairy, sugar-free soy or almond milk
- Cheese: unprocessed cheddar, parmesan, ricotta, cottage cheese and quark. For those with a sensitive gut, try goat's and sheep's cheese (like manchego)
- Chicken*: free range and organic if possible
- Eggs: free range and organic if possible
- Fish*: cold-water fatty fish such as trout, salmon, cod, halibut, sardines, sole and blue-eye trevalla. Eat no more than two tins of tinned tuna a week due to its mercury content; wild-caught fish is best

- Legumes: see page 138. Legumes are both a smart carb and a protein
- Nuts: see below
- Pork: preferably free range if possible
- Red meat: grass-fed and organic if possible
- Seeds (raw or dry roasted): pumpkin, sesame, sunflower and flaxseeds
- Soy: organic GMO-free tofu, miso paste
- Miso soup: not a huge source of protein, but good to keep in the pantry as a low-sugar snack
- Yoghurt: plain goat's or sheep's milk yoghurt, or plain full-fat Greek-style yoghurt

Nuts & seeds

For a simple healthy snack, or to add crunch to a salad, pesto or crumble, it's always great to have some raw or dry-roasted nuts on hand. I usually have almonds and pine nuts, while pistachios, walnuts, hazelnuts and macadamias make an appearance from time to time. If you need to pad out a meal with additional protein, seeds and nuts are a fantastic, nutrient-dense choice. Store them in the fridge to extend their shelf life.

*Keep a few fish fillets or chicken thighs or breasts in your freezer – you never know when you might need them. Ask your butcher to vacuum-seal them and they'll keep in the freezer for months.

LEGUMES

High in fibre and minerals and a great source of protein,
legumes are inexpensive and have a long shelf life, making
them a perfect pantry staple. They're great in salads or to bulk
out soups, stews, pasta sauces and curries.
Remember, too, that legumes are also a smart carb, so have
them at lunchtime rather than dinner if you are trying to lose
weight. Their abundant fibre content has a two-fold effect on
our weight. Firstly, they make us feel full and satisfied and,
secondly, they keep our 'pipes' moving along nicely.

- Beans – such as adzuki, black, butter, cannellini, kidney, soy and pinto beans
- Lentils* – any variety
- Peas – such as chickpeas*, split peas, black-eyed peas

My favourite lentils are the little dark-green French ones, known as puy lentils, as they are very forgiving and don't turn to mush like other lentils do. Cook and top with a poached egg for a perfect meal! And while there's no shortage of tinned legumes on the market, if I had to narrow down to one essential, chickpeas would be it. A meal in a can, chickpeas are an excellent source of protein and iron. Use them to bulk out curries, soups and pasta sauces, or simply add them to a salad.

SPICES & SEASONINGS

I love experimenting with spices – it's one of the great joys of cooking. Imagine a warm bowl of oats without the warming scent of cinnamon, or a curry without that earthy whiff of turmeric. Go crazy and invest in any spice or seasoning that intrigues you; this is how you add flavour and flair to your meals. Having chicken three nights a week sounds boring, but when you add paprika one night for a Mexican dish, or Chinese five-spice another night for an oriental feel, or rosemary and oregano for an Italian twist, things get a lot more exciting.

Choose spices free of preservatives, additives and colours. Some spice mixes contain a little sugar, but when spread over many meals, the impact is insignificant. All herbs are on the menu, too, and taste great fresh from your own garden.

Here are some of my favourite seasonings.

- Black pepper
- Chilli
- Curry pastes
- Dulse flakes – a wonderfully salty, iodine-rich seaweed sprinkle
- Extracts – vanilla, peppermint, mint
- Fish sauce
- Garlic – but not imported, as imported garlic is fumigated with methyl bromide, and often bleached
- Ginger
- Liquid aminos – gluten-free alternative to soy sauce
- Monkfruit powder – natural sugar substitute
- Mustards – French, English, seeded
- Oyster sauce
- Paprika – sweet, hot and/or smoked
- Pure food flavour extracts – mint, orange, coconut, lemon, etc
- Salt – Celtic, Himalayan or sea salt
- Stevia – a natural sugar substitute
- Tamari – a salty and sassy Japanese soy sauce, usually wheat-free
- Vanilla bean paste

OTHER BRILLIANT PANTRY ESSENTIALS

Almond flour – tasty and packed with protein, almond flour can be used in biscuits, cakes and bread-making

Anchovies – add them to your next soup or stew, to enhance the umami flavours of meat

Capers – these add a burst of bright saltiness to any meal

Cocoa powder – great for hot chocolates and for baking

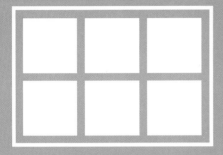

Dark chocolate – always keep some good-quality dark chocolate tucked away for emergencies; it's perfect for dessert when you haven't prepared anything for guests

Dried fruit – fabulous in a salad, or add to your oats. Just watch your serving size!

Preserved lemons – another little ray of salty sunshine that adds a zing of brine to any meal

Tinned tomatoes – inexpensive, versatile and with a great shelf life, with tinned tomatoes you always have the beginnings of a meal. Use them in pasta sauces, to add richness to soups or stews or as a bed in which to bake eggs

Vinegar – I keep some balsamic or sherry vinegar for salads; rice wine vinegar for Asian recipes; and some red wine or white wine vinegar for dressings and marinades

Kitchen essentials

If you only gained your cooking knowledge from *MasterChef* or gourmet food magazines, you'd probably think that, in order to cook well, you need to have access to a blast freezer, a sous-vide machine, seven types of gelatine and at least one jar of freeze-dried powdered pomegranate.

Well, that's simply not true. Even if you have a teeny-weeny apartment kitchen, you can still whip up your own perfectly delicious, healthy meals, economically and efficiently.

Here are my favourite hard-working kitchen items that make light work of preparing a whole range of dishes.

Knives: Forget the block sets, all you need is a good-quality cook's knife and a bread knife.

Chopping board: Opt for one large wooden board for all-purpose chopping, and a plastic one (for raw meat and poultry) that can go in the dishwasher.

Utensils: A spiraliser (for making vegetable ribbons), vegetable peeler, whisk, tin opener, spatula (more versatile than tongs) and microplane (for finely grating anything from cheese to chocolate).

Salad/mixing bowls: Invest in a set of mixing bowls that can also be used for serving salads.

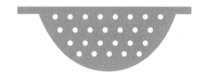

Large fine-mesh strainer: For draining pasta, sieving flour and removing lumps from sauces or custard.

Frying pan: A medium-sized frying pan, with an ovenproof handle so you can start cooking on the stovetop and then finish your dish in the oven.

Pots: At least one medium-sized pot (I like cast iron) for boiling pasta, making soups and even slow-cooking.

Roasting dish: You don't need to buy separate baking trays – you can use the one roasting dish for baking cookies and scones, cooking a lasagne in, and of course your lamb roast. Invest in a cast-iron one and it'll last forever.

Storage canisters and glass containers: Leftover food will stay fresher for longer when stored properly. Choose glass over plastic, as there is some research to suggest the chemicals in plastic can leach into your food.

A barbecue: Not strictly essential, but it sure does make summer enjoyable!

5

The 28-day eating plan

Week
One

You're curious and ready, otherwise you wouldn't have made it this far! So, here are a few helpful ideas for the first week to help you prepare for the small changes you'll make. You truly can eat delicious food, enjoy a glass or two of wine – and still maintain or lose weight.

During the first week, you may find the way of eating that is being spelt out in this book a little odd. Why? Because while the food and meals are really delicious, they are actually very low in sugar (even natural sugars), low in gluten, and free of 'franken foods' or preservatives – so your body may need a period of adjustment if you are used to a different way of eating.

The key to making small changes in your wellness is preparation. So, concentrate on preparing your kitchen and pantry and filling your fridge the first week.

- Look through the dinner recipes on the following pages, think about your breakfasts and lunches and map out your week.
- Make a detailed shopping list, shop and do any food prep for the week.

- Every night, take 10 minutes to sketch out what you want your tomorrow to look like. Keep it simple. It only needs to make sense to you, and speak to your true desire for a change. For example, when I first started doing this I would draw a bridge next to the small changes I knew were going to be big for me to cross – my note to myself that made sense to me!
- I often find that people who partner up with a buddy succeed at creating sustainable new habits, so why not find a wellness buddy to do this with? Who could that be? Can you pause for a minute and text them right now?

THE 28-DAY EATING PLAN **147**

LEMONY ROAST VEG & CHICKPEA SALAD

Here's your chance to enjoy a fast roast veggie dinner that's just as satisfying and delicious as a meaty one. Chickpeas are great for low-carb munchers like us who also want plenty of protein. They are an excellent source of fibre, vitamins and minerals, and don't cause your blood sugar to spike because they are slow burners. As they take longer to digest, they provide us with a satisfying feeling of fullness.

SERVES 4 ♥ PREPARATION TIME: **20 MINS** COOKING TIME: **35 MINS**

2 sweet potatoes, halved then cut into wedges

3 red onions, unpeeled, cut into wedges

1 head cauliflower, broken into bite-sized florets

1 head broccoli, broken into bite-sized florets

8 garlic cloves, unpeeled

8 basil sprigs

½ cup extra virgin olive oil

¼ cup lemon juice

1 tablespoon raw honey

2 teaspoons cumin seeds, toasted

1 x 400 g tin chickpeas, drained and rinsed

200 g baby spinach or rocket

finely grated zest of 1 lemon

sea salt and freshly ground black pepper

Preheat the oven to 200°C (180°C fan-forced). Line a roasting tin with baking paper.

Toss together the sweet potato, onion, cauliflower, broccoli, garlic, half the basil and half the olive oil and spread out in a single layer in the prepared tin. Roast for 35 minutes.

Whisk together the lemon juice, honey, cumin and remaining olive oil in a large bowl and toss through the chickpeas. Gently fold in all the roasted veggies except the onion.

Arrange the spinach or rocket on a platter and layer on the roasted veg and chickpeas. Peel the onion into petals and scatter over the top. Sprinkle over the lemon zest and the remaining basil, and season with salt and pepper, if desired.

BULK IT UP: *Add some barbecued chicken or steak on the side.*

UP THE PROTEIN: *Sprinkle toasted pumpkin seeds over the top for additional protein and zinc.*

UP THE FIBRE: *Sprinkle whole flaxseeds into the bowl when tossing the salad.*

FOR CHEESE LOVERS: *Throw in some crumbled goat's cheese or pan-fried haloumi.*

CREAMY VEGETABLE SOUP

I love cream and I love veggies so when I can combine them both in a soup I do. But the tastebud explosion here is not cream at all … it is the creaminess of cashews, making it a lighter meal than you might expect, but still packed with protein and nutrients. Enjoy it just as it is, or sprinkle over your choice of fresh herbs.

SERVES 4 ♥ PREPARATION TIME: **15 MINS** COOKING TIME: **30 MINS**

1 cup raw unsalted cashews
2 tablespoons coconut oil or
    extra virgin olive oil
1 large brown onion,
    roughly chopped
2 garlic cloves,
    roughly chopped
5 cups chopped broccoli,
    cauliflower and/or carrots
3–4 cups vegetable stock
    or water
2 teaspoons sea salt
1–2 teaspoons cayenne pepper
    (to taste)
coriander sprigs, to serve

Soak the cashews in water for 15 minutes, then drain.

Meanwhile, heat the oil in a large saucepan over medium heat, add the onion and garlic and cook for 5 minutes or until softened. Add the vegetables and enough stock or water to cover, then season with the salt and cayenne pepper. Bring to the boil, then reduce the heat to low and simmer for 20 minutes or until the vegetables are tender.

Add the drained cashews, then blend with a stick blender (or in an upright blender) until smooth.

Divide among four bowls and serve hot garnished with coriander.

DITCH THE NUTS: *If you don't eat nuts, add 200 ml coconut milk just before blending (heat it through at a simmer over low heat otherwise it will separate).*

BULK IT UP: *Add a drained 400 g tin of chickpeas or legumes of your choice after blending and simmer for 10 minutes. Remember legumes are both a carb and a protein so go easy on them at dinner.*

SPICE IT UP: *Add a pinch of smoked paprika, chilli powder or jalapeno pepper powder.*

MEXICAN FISH BOWL

Packed with colourful vegetables and vitamin- and phytonutrient-rich prebiotic beans and soft white fish, these burrito bowls are perfect for a summer dinner party or a family dinner. The guacamole is infinitely adaptable. You could add finely diced tomato, red onion or garlic, a handful of chopped coriander, or a dash of Tabasco or cayenne pepper for spice.

SERVES 4 ♥ PREPARATION TIME: 20 MINS COOKING TIME: 15 MINS

2 corn cobs, husks and
   silks removed
melted butter, for brushing
1 x 400 g tin black beans,
   drained and rinsed
½ red capsicum, seeded
   and diced
1 Lebanese cucumber, diced
½ red onion, diced
a handful of cherry
   tomatoes, quartered or
   1 large tomato, diced
1 teaspoon sweet paprika
½ bunch coriander, leaves
   picked and finely chopped,
   plus extra leaves to serve
splash of extra virgin olive oil
sea salt and freshly ground
   black pepper
2 ripe avocados
juice of 1 lemon or 2 limes,
   plus extra wedges, to serve
3 tablespoons coconut oil,
   extra virgin olive oil
   or butter
700 g firm white fish fillets
   (such as flathead, snapper,
   whiting or dory), skin and
   bones removed
1 cos (romaine) lettuce,
   shredded
natural yoghurt, to serve

Heat a barbecue grill plate to medium–hot. Lightly brush the corn cobs with butter and cook on the barbecue, turning often, for 5–8 minutes or until tender and charred in spots. Set aside to cool, then cut off the kernels with a sharp knife.

Meanwhile, place the beans, capsicum, corn, cucumber, onion, tomato, paprika, coriander and a splash of olive oil in a bowl. Season the salsa with salt and pepper and toss to combine.

Using a fork, mash the avocado flesh with the lemon or lime juice. Season to taste.

Heat the oil or butter in a large frying pan over high heat. Add the fish fillets and cook for 1–2 minutes each side or until just cooked through. Gently break into bite-sized pieces.

To serve, scatter the shredded lettuce over a large plate or platter and arrange the fish, black bean salsa, guacamole and yoghurt on top. Scatter with extra coriander and lemon or lime wedges, then take to the table and let everyone help themselves.

FOR CARB-LOVING FAMILY MEMBERS: *Use a taco shell, tortillas or a burrito wrap.*
CHANGE UP THE BEANS: *Butter beans or chickpeas are also great.*
SWAP THE HERBS: *Not a fan of coriander? Try mint or basil.*
SPICE IT UP: *Experiment! Have a look at which spices you have and give something new a go.*
TIME POOR? *Use frozen baby corn kernels instead of fresh corn.*

MEATBALLS WITH RAGU & ZOODLES

I love the comforting warmth of a slow-cooked ragu but if you are time poor (as I often am), it's fine to use a good-quality bought tomato sauce instead of making your own. This version is decidedly lighter than the hearty stews a discerning nonna would make, but it has all the flavour you'd expect and more. I love serving this for Sunday lunch with friends, or for a nourishing weeknight dinner.

SERVES 4 ♥ PREPARATION TIME: 25 MINS COOKING TIME: 35 MINS

1 kg tomatoes, halved

1½ tablespoons extra virgin olive oil, plus extra for drizzling

1 brown onion, finely diced

2 garlic cloves, crushed

1 carrot, finely diced

1 celery stalk, finely diced

3 tablespoons tomato paste

1 tablespoon finely chopped thyme leaves

½ cup vegetable stock

1 tablespoon finely chopped oregano leaves

¼ bunch basil, leaves picked

4 zucchini, spiralised

1 tablespoon balsamic vinegar

sea salt and freshly ground black pepper

TURKEY MEATBALLS

400 g turkey mince

400 g chicken thigh mince (it's important you use thigh meat as it stops the meatballs from drying out)

2 tablespoons finely chopped oregano leaves

2 tablespoons finely chopped flat-leaf parsley leaves

2 tablespoons pitted green olives, chopped

2 garlic cloves, crushed

3 tablespoons grated parmesan

2 eggs, lightly beaten

2 tablespoons rice breadcrumbs

RECIPE CONTINUED >

Preheat the oven to 220°C (200°C fan-forced) and line a large baking tray with baking paper.

Spread out the tomatoes on the prepared tray and drizzle lightly with olive oil. Roast for 30 minutes or until soft and collapsed. Allow to cool slightly, then purée until smooth.

Heat the remaining olive oil in a large frying pan over medium heat. Add the onion, garlic, carrot and celery and cook for a few minutes or until softened. Stir in the tomato paste and thyme.

Add the stock, oregano, most of the basil (leaving a few leaves to garnish) and the puréed tomato and bring to the boil, then reduce the heat to low and simmer for 1 hour.

Meanwhile, to make the meatballs, combine the turkey and chicken mince, oregano, parsley, olives, garlic and parmesan in a bowl. Add the egg and then the rice breadcrumbs, ensuring everything is evenly mixed.

Preheat the oven to 200°C (180°C fan-forced) and line a baking tray with baking paper.

Roll the mince mixture into golf ball–sized balls and place on the prepared tray. Refrigerate for 15 minutes.

Place the meatballs in the oven and reduce the temperature to 180°C (160°C fan-forced). Bake for 10 minutes or until cooked through.

Meanwhile, briefly blanch the zoodles until tender.

Remove the sauce from the heat and stir in the balsamic vinegar. Stir through the meatballs and season to taste.

Divide the zoodles among four bowls and serve with the meatballs and ragu on top.

CHANGE UP THE PROTEIN: *Omit the turkey mince and use 800 g chicken mince, or try a mix of half pork and half beef mince. Lamb is good too. In fact, any mince will do!*

FOR CARB-LOVING FAMILY MEMBERS: *Serve with pasta.*

BEEF FILLET TRAYBAKE

I love a one-tray dinner — mainly because I love cooking, but I don't love cleaning up. I usually prepare the marinade the night before so the flavours can really soak in while I'm at work. If you like this marinade, double or triple it next time for future meals. And use up whatever veggies you have in the crisper drawer — the real key here is that delicious sauce!

SERVES 4 ♥ PREPARATION TIME: 20 MINS + MARINATING COOKING TIME: 30 MINS + RESTING

1 x 650 g beef fillet,
  sliced into thin strips
1 red onion, sliced
1 large sweet potato, quartered
  and cut into thin wedges
2 teaspoons extra virgin
  olive oil
1 teaspoon sea salt
2 red capsicums, seeded and
  cut into strips
1 bunch asparagus, trimmed
  and chopped
1 zucchini, cut into
  bite-sized pieces
1 teaspoon freshly ground
  black pepper

MARINADE
½ cup balsamic vinegar
4 garlic cloves, finely chopped
1 teaspoon chopped
  rosemary leaves
½ teaspoon sea salt
½ teaspoon freshly ground
  black pepper
2 teaspoons dijon mustard
½ cup extra virgin olive oil

To make the marinade, blend the vinegar, garlic, rosemary, salt, pepper and mustard until combined. Slowly drizzle in the olive oil and whisk until emulsified. Divide the mixture in half and set aside.

Place the beef strips in a bowl and pour over half the marinade. Turn to coat and set aside. (If you are marinating the beef for a few hours or overnight, cover the bowl with plastic film and place in the fridge.)

Preheat the oven to 200°C (180°C fan-forced). Oil a large roasting tin and place in the oven to preheat.

Coat the onion and sweet potato with 1 teaspoon olive oil and season with ½ teaspoon salt. Roast in the preheated tin for 10 minutes.

Coat the capsicum, asparagus and zucchini with the remaining oil and season with pepper and the remaining salt. Add to the tin and roast for a further 10–15 minutes or until all the vegetables are cooked.

Preheat the oven grill to hot.

Move the vegetables to the outer edges of the tin (making sure there is still space between them so they become crisp and caramelised; it's better to use two tins if you don't have one tin large enough). Arrange the marinated beef in a single layer in the centre and place under the grill for 5 minutes, then turn the beef and vegetables over and grill for a further 3 minutes.

Allow the beef to rest for 5 minutes, then serve with the vegetables and the remaining marinade on the side.

CHANGE UP THE PROTEIN: *Replace the beef with lamb or pork.*
FOR CARB-LOVING FAMILY MEMBERS: *Add more sweet potato.*
NUTRIENT BOOST: *Add a side salad of your choice.*

THAI GOODNESS BOWL

These days, everyone and their mother is into goodness bowls and nourish bowls and heaven knows what other kinds of bowl. I get it, of course; who doesn't want to sit down and eat something that's not only Instagram pretty but also really, really good for you? Well, that's what laksa is: a bowl packed with nutrition and amazing flavours and, yep, it looks pretty great too. My version is light on carbs and heavy on vegetables (zucchini noodles), protein and good fats in the form of coconut milk, which gives us a feeling of satiety (stopping us from bingeing later!). What's more, coconut is a medium-chain triglyceride, which means the body sees this fat as a fuel and will often burn it the same way it burns carbs — that is, for energy. Sleeves up, chopsticks at the ready: it's time to laksa.

SERVES 4 ♥ PREPARATION TIME: **15 MINS** COOKING TIME: **20 MINS**

4 medium zucchini, spiralised,
    or 2 x 400 g packets
    konjac noodles
sea salt
1 bird's eye chilli, seeded and
    thinly sliced
1 x 185 g jar laksa paste
2 x 400 ml tins coconut milk
4 chicken thigh fillets, diced
1 bunch gai larn or bok choy,
    thinly sliced
400 g green beans, trimmed
    and finely chopped
basil leaves, to serve

Sprinkle the spiralised zucchini with sea salt and set aside while you make the soup. If you're using konjac noodles, drain the water out, then place them in boiling water for 2 minutes. Drain.

Combine the chilli, laksa paste and coconut milk in a medium saucepan and bring to a simmer. Add the chicken and cook over low heat for about 6 minutes or until the chicken is cooked through. Add the vegetables and cook for another 3 minutes until tender.

Add the spiralised zucchini or konjac noodles to the pan and bring back to a simmer. Taste and season with salt if necessary. Ladle the soup into four deep bowls and top with basil leaves to serve.

GO VEGETARIAN: *Replace the chicken with chickpeas or GMO-free firm tofu.*
FOR CARB-LOVING FAMILY MEMBERS: *Replace the zucchini noodles with rice noodles or serve with steamed jasmine rice.*
SWAP THE HERBS: *Herbs can be polarising, so choose the ones you love best. Mint, coriander and Thai basil also work well here.*
NUTRIENT BOOST: *You could add plenty of chopped fresh or frozen veg here: red capsicum, snow peas, carrots, bean sprouts and cauliflower all work beautifully. Simply add the veg with the coconut milk and water and simmer for a few minutes until cooked.*

NUTTY CHICKEN SCHNITZ

As an honorary Australian, I feel it's my civic duty to eat as many macadamias as humanly possible – they are incredibly delicious and so good for you. Packed with omega-7 fatty oils and palmitoleic acid, which can curb hunger and keep you hydrated too, macadamias are a bit of a wonder of nature. Similar to the healthy fats found in avocados and olive oil, macadamias are a rich source of monounsaturated fats, which help to reduce cholesterol and triglycerides in the body, supporting a healthy heart.

In this reimagining of that classic pub dish, the ground macadamias and mustard add crunch and a welcome touch of richness.

SERVES 4 ♥ PREPARATION TIME: 15 MINS COOKING TIME: 25 MINS

4 chicken breast fillets
  (about 800 g)
1 cup raw unsalted macadamias
⅓ cup finely chopped chives
sea salt and freshly ground
  black pepper
2 tablespoons dijon mustard
2 cups green beans,
  sliced horizontally
3 cups baby spinach
2 tablespoons olive oil
2 tablespoons lemon juice
1 teaspoon toasted cumin
  seeds, lightly crushed
3 tablespoons toasted
  pumpkin seeds
3 teaspoons poppy seeds

Preheat the oven to 200°C (180°C fan-forced). Line a large baking tray with baking paper.

Use a rolling pin to lightly beat the chicken breasts to an even thickness, then set aside.

Place the macadamias in a food processor and roughly pulse (don't take them too far; aim for a rubble-like texture rather than breadcrumbs). Transfer to a bowl, stir in half the chives and season with salt and pepper.

Place the flattened chicken breasts on the prepared tray and spread evenly with the mustard. Press the macadamia mixture onto the mustard, and bake for 25 minutes or until golden and cooked through.

Meanwhile, combine the beans, spinach, olive oil, lemon juice and seeds in a large bowl and gently toss together.

Serve the greens with the chicken schnitz, sprinkled with the remaining chives.

GO NUTS: *While I could wax lyrical about macadamias for days, any kind of nut will work here. Pecans are especially great.*
FOR CARB-LOVING FAMILY MEMBERS: *Serve with mashed sweet potato or roast potatoes.*
NUTRIENT BOOST: *Add any side vegetable to this meal, especially if it's something green.*

Week
Two

Feeling a new rhythm? Less bloated? By the end of week 2, a new pattern will set in. You will be looking forward to seeking out the next lot of recipes for the week and preparing them.

Why does this feel so different from every other 'diet' you've done before?

Because it's not a diet or a cleanse. It's going to be your new way of life – one full of abundance, rather than deprivation.

Now that you're getting your food into a rhythm, can you begin to focus on what micro habits you can implement?

- Remember, please don't introduce more than one or two micro habits a week.
- The word *micro* is imperative, as we know from extensive research that it is the small changes that become sustainable, because they are not overwhelming or too far-fetched.

Review the list of micro habits starting on page 75 and perhaps begin with my favourite one: banishing guilt. Stop punishing yourself about what you may have done to yourself, or your weight, or how you ate [insert whatever] a few months ago or any of that nonsense. Today is a new day. You're here, reading this

book, entering your second week, and thinking to yourself, 'Hey, this isn't too difficult at all. I can do this!'

Perhaps after reviewing the list of micro habits, you might have some of your own thoughts on things you need to change, and you now want to add them into your journey. Things that have challenged you in the past, but have been too big to break or give up?

One of my clients wanted to start moving more due to his office desk job. He didn't like the idea of buying an expensive fitness tracker, but loved the free Health app on his mobile phone. He committed to 8,000 steps a day, and if he didn't get there, he pushed himself to go for a walk after dinner. Nice! A perfect micro habit that helped him exercise more.

Always remember: small steps can have lasting results.

SCRUMPTIOUS FISHCAKES

Quick, simple and incredibly tasty, these Thai fishcakes are great for an easy weeknight dinner, or make a wonderful addition to lunchboxes. Packed with herbs and vegetables which aid immune support, clear congestion and support bone health, these delicious morsels are also a great source of protein, B vitamins, iodine and essential fatty acids from the fish. In my experience, most things in the shape of a muffin are inviting, so even the fussiest of eaters like these — give them a go!

SERVES **4** ♥ PREPARATION TIME: **15 MINS** COOKING TIME: **15 MINS**

1 tablespoon olive oil

1 avocado

sea salt and freshly ground
   black pepper

lime wedges, to serve

sweet chilli sauce (preferably
   low sugar), to taste

FISHCAKES

700 g firm white fish fillets
   (such as flathead, snapper,
   whiting or dory), skin
   and bones removed,
   roughly diced

2 tablespoons coconut cream

1 teaspoon fish sauce

2 teaspoons green curry paste

1 bunch coriander, stems and
   leaves chopped

1 tablespoon lime juice

2 teaspoons chopped ginger

2 spring onions, white part
   only, chopped

2 garlic cloves, chopped

Preheat the oven to 180°C (160°C fan-forced). Grease eight holes of a standard muffin tin with the olive oil.

To make the fishcakes, place all the ingredients in a food processor and blitz to a medium coarse texture.

Divide the mixture evenly among the prepared muffin holes, filling them only three-quarters full. Bake for 15 minutes or until firm and cooked through. Rest on a wire rack.

Meanwhile, mash the avocado flesh and season with salt and pepper.

Serve the fishcakes with the mashed avocado, lime wedges and sweet chilli sauce.

MAKE IT A NEW MEAL: *Turn these muffins into meatballs and toss through konjac noodles dressed in sesame oil and lime juice.*
FOR CARB-LOVING FAMILY MEMBERS: *Make the patties bigger and serve on wholegrain buns as burgers.*

ROASTED & RAW SALAD BOWL

Hot salad! Well this one is hot because it's trendy but it's also served warm. It actually started life as an accident but quickly turned into a family favourite. I usually roast veggies and let them cool for hours before tossing them through seasonal raw veggies and herbs, but on one occasion I didn't have the time so I just tossed them in warm. It was delicious – so full of flavour and abundant in vitamins and fibre. I always double the quantities when I make a dressing so I can use it over the next few days in other meals.

SERVES 4 ♥ PREPARATION TIME: **20 MINS** COOKING TIME: **40 MINS**

2 large sweet potatoes,
    scrubbed but not peeled,
    cut into bite-sized cubes
3 tablespoons extra virgin
    olive oil
1 head cauliflower, broken into
    florets
2 red onions, each cut into 8
    wedges
2 handfuls of baby spinach
1 bunch mint, leaves picked
1 bunch coriander, leaves
    picked (reserve the roots
    for the dressing)
finely grated zest of 2 lemons
    (reserve the juice for the
    dressing)

DRESSING
juice of 2 lemons
½ cup extra virgin olive oil
roots from 1 bunch coriander,
    finely chopped
1 long red chilli, seeds
    removed, thinly sliced
sea salt and freshly ground
    black pepper

Preheat the oven to 220°C (200°C fan-forced). Line two baking trays with baking paper.

Spread the sweet potato over one of the prepared trays and drizzle with some of the olive oil. Spread the cauliflower and onion over the second tray and drizzle with the remaining olive oil. Gently toss to coat.

Reduce the oven temperature to 180°C (160°C fan-forced). Place the tray of sweet potato in the oven and roast for 20 minutes. Add the cauliflower and onion and roast for a further 20 minutes or until all the vegetables are tender.

Meanwhile, to make the dressing, place all the ingredients in a glass jar and shake well to combine.

Place the spinach, mint and coriander leaves in a large bowl. Add the warm roasted vegetables and toss through half the dressing.

Divide the salad among bowls and sprinkle over the lemon zest. Offer the remaining dressing for those who might like extra.

PROTEIN BOOST: *Add a piece of red meat, fish or chicken, or slice some hard-boiled eggs over the top.*
GO NUTS: *Sprinkle roasted pine nuts over the top.*
UP THE FIBRE: *Sprinkle whole flaxseeds into the bowl when tossing the salad.*
FOR CHEESE LOVERS: *Throw in some crumbled goat's cheese or pan-fried haloumi.*

MISO-GLAZED SALMON

The salty, savoury flavour of miso instantly takes me to Japan, even if I'm doing nothing more exotic than sitting at my dining room table with my family. I love this meal for so many reasons: it's quick, it's simple, and you can adapt it in so many ways. While I don't love the term 'superfood', salmon and ocean trout are both worthy of the title; they are full of protein and good-quality fats, which stabilise blood sugar and keep us satisfied. Serve it with noodles or rice to make it more substantial, add whatever greens or vegetables you have on hand, and top it with dulse flakes, sesame seeds or finely chopped roasted seaweed sheets.

SERVES 4 ♥ PREPARATION TIME: **15 MINS + MARINATING** COOKING TIME: **10 MINS**

2 tablespoons white
   miso paste
3 tablespoons boiling water
3 tablespoons pure
   maple syrup
¼ cup sesame oil
¼ cup grated ginger
4 x 175 g salmon fillets, skin
   and bones removed (ocean
   trout is also great here)
1 tablespoon tamari
4 cups chopped Asian greens
   (such as bok choy, choy sum
   and broccolini)
1 teaspoon black sesame seeds
½ cup coriander
1 bird's eye chilli, thinly sliced

Preheat the oven to 180°C (160°C fan-forced). Line a baking tray with baking paper.

Place the miso paste in a large heatproof bowl, pour in the boiling water and whisk to make a thin paste. Add the maple syrup, 2 tablespoons of the sesame oil and half the ginger and whisk again to combine. Add the salmon to the bowl and rub the glaze into the fillets. Set aside to marinate for at least 15 minutes (the longer, the better).

Spread out the salmon on the prepared tray and spoon over the remaining glaze. Transfer to the oven and bake for 10 minutes or until the fish is cooked through.

Meanwhile, combine the tamari and remaining sesame oil and ginger in a large frying pan over medium heat. Add the greens and toss for a few minutes or until cooked to your liking.

Divide the salmon and greens among serving plates and garnish with the sesame seeds, coriander and chilli.

CHANGE UP THE PROTEIN: *Use any type of fish fillet you like.*
GO VEGETARIAN: *Use GMO-free firm tofu.*
FOR CARB-LOVING FAMILY MEMBERS: *Serve with nutrient-dense brown rice or soba noodles.*

LAMB & HALOUMI MEATBALLS

Taste-sensation overload! You'll want to triple this recipe. The key ingredient here is haloumi — it makes the meatballs stick together, plus it adds flavour and texture. Don't worry about making your own chermoula, buy a quality one from a greengrocer. Marinades like chermoula go so well with meat and fish; you'll be happy to eat low-carb as the flavours are so satisfying.

SERVES **4** ♥ PREPARATION TIME: **15 MINS** COOKING TIME: **30 MINS**

½ cup regular or gluten-free
   breadcrumbs
2 teaspoons A2 milk
600 g lamb mince
250 g haloumi, grated
¼ cup chermoula
1 teaspoon freshly ground
   black pepper
⅓ cup extra virgin olive oil
½ large brown onion,
   finely diced
4 garlic cloves, finely chopped
1 teaspoon ground turmeric
½ teaspoon dried thyme leaves
¼ teaspoon ground coriander
2 x 400 g tins diced tomatoes
¼ cup sherry vinegar
2 teaspoons brown sugar
flat-leaf parsley leaves,
   to serve

Preheat the oven to 200°C (180°C fan-forced).

Place the breadcrumbs and milk in a large bowl and mix together so the breadcrumbs soak up the milk. Add the lamb, haloumi, chermoula and pepper and combine thoroughly with your hands. Roll the mixture into balls slightly smaller than a golf ball.

Heat half the oil in a frying pan over medium–high heat and, working in batches, cook the meatballs until just browned. As you've finished each batch, transfer them to a baking paper–lined tray. Once all the meatballs are browned, pop them in the oven for 10 minutes or until cooked through.

Meanwhile, heat the remaining oil over medium heat in the same frying pan you cooked the meatballs in. Add the onion and cook for 2–3 minutes or until softened. Add the garlic and cook, stirring, for 1–2 minutes. Add the turmeric, thyme and coriander and cook for a further minute, scraping the bottom of the pan to ensure nothing catches.

Add the tomatoes, vinegar and sugar to the pan and cook for 15 minutes, stirring occasionally. Toss in the cooked meatballs and cook for another 5 minutes, gently folding all the ingredients together. Serve immediately, scattered with flat-leaf parsley.

FOR CARB-LOVING FAMILY MEMBERS: *Serve on a bed of sweet potato mash.*
VEGGIE BOOST: *Finely grate ½ head cauliflower, sauté briefly in olive oil and serve with the meatballs (as pictured opposite).*

FRI-YAY TACOS WITH ZUCCHINI TORTILLAS

At the end of the working week, it's nice to celebrate with a fun (but simple!) meal. Add plenty of vegetables — such as diced capsicum and tomato, or grilled corn — to round out this winning dish. And if you like to live it up, serve with a glass of tequila, lime and soda. Hey, it's Friday!

SERVES 4 ♥ PREPARATION TIME: **20 MINS** COOKING TIME: **35 MINS**

2 tablespoons extra virgin
    olive oil
1 red onion, diced
4 garlic cloves, crushed
800 g beef rump or scotch
    fillet, diced into 3 cm pieces
½ cup tomato paste
3 teaspoons smoked paprika
    (or Mexican spice mix)
sea salt and freshly ground
    black pepper
chilli flakes, to taste
1 cup grated cheddar
coriander leaves and
    chopped cos (romaine)
    lettuce, to serve
ZUCCHINI TORTILLAS
2 large zucchini
    (about 300 g), grated
½ cup grated parmesan
⅔ cup almond meal
2 eggs, lightly beaten
½ teaspoon sea salt

Preheat the oven to 200°C (180°C fan-forced). Line two large baking trays with baking paper.

To make the tortillas, mix together all the ingredients in a bowl. Using an ice-cream scoop, scoop out 12 even portions and place on the prepared trays. Flatten them out into 8 cm circles. Bake for 20–25 minutes or until golden and cooked through.

Meanwhile, heat the olive oil in a frying pan over medium heat, add the onion and cook for 5 minutes until softened and lightly golden. Add the garlic and cook, stirring, for 2–3 minutes. Remove the onion and garlic from the pan and set aside. Increase the heat to high and, working in batches, cook the beef for 2–3 minutes until browned.

Return the onion and garlic to the pan. Add the tomato paste, paprika and 3 tablespoons water and simmer, stirring, for 5 minutes or until the beef is cooked to your liking. Season generously with salt, pepper and chilli flakes.

Serve the beef and tortillas with the cheddar, coriander and lettuce.

GO VEGETARIAN: *Replace the beef with tempeh or firm tofu.*
ROUND IT OUT: *Add a good dollop of sour cream or guacamole.*
FUN FOOD ADDITION: *Add some charred corn on the cob with melted butter and chilli salt.*

MEXICAN CHICKEN BURGERS

Okay, okay, so you probably didn't expect to see a recipe for a spicy burger in here. There's a misconception that these foods are 'bad' for you, but it's not true. Chilli is what we nutritionists call a thermogenic food — it boosts our metabolic rate, even at rest. So by using Mexican spices and adding plenty of fresh vegetables and good-quality protein, we can take what's normally seen as an indulgent meal and make it perfect for everyday eating.

I use Herbie's taco seasoning, which is available online. It contains sweet paprika, cumin, sea salt, smoked paprika, coriander seed and leaf, amchur (green mango powder), chilli, cinnamon and oregano. You can substitute with your own mix of these spices or another taco seasoning mix.

SERVES **4** ♥ PREPARATION TIME: **15 MINS** COOKING TIME: **10 MINS**

1 tablespoon extra virgin olive oil

1 avocado

ZESTY SALSA

1 cup chopped coriander leaves

2 garlic cloves,
 roughly chopped

½ red onion, diced

1 jalapeno chilli, finely chopped

500 g ripe cherry tomatoes,
 quartered

finely grated zest and juice
 of 1 lime

pinch of sea salt

CHICKEN PATTIES

700 g chicken mince

1¼ tablespoons taco seasoning

6 spring onions, white part only,
 thinly sliced

1 egg

½ cup grated cheddar

1 teaspoon ground coriander

1 jalapeno chilli, finely chopped

sea salt and freshly ground
 black pepper

To make the salsa, place the coriander, garlic and onion in a food processor and blitz for 1 minute. Then combine the chilli, tomato, lime zest and juice and salt in a bowl. Add the mixture from the food processor and stir well to combine.

For the patties, place all the ingredients in a large bowl and mix until combined. Form the mixture into four burger-style patties.

Heat the olive oil in a large non-stick frying pan (or barbecue plate) over medium heat. Add the patties and cook for 4–5 minutes each side or until cooked through.

Meanwhile, mash the avocado flesh and season with salt and pepper.

Serve the patties with the smashed avocado and zesty salsa.

MAKE IT CRUNCHY: *Add chopped fennel or celery to your salsa.*

MAKE IT QUICK: *Skip the homemade guacamole and salsa; instead, slice an avocado and serve with store-bought salsa.*

GO PESCATARIAN: *Use white fish fillets instead of chicken. Ask your fishmonger to mince it, or do it yourself in a food processor.*

NUTRIENT BOOST: *Bulk up your salsa with roasted chopped almonds and add extra vegetables to your plate — cauliflower rice, steamed broccoli and mashed sweet potato work well.*

FOR CARB-LOVING FAMILY MEMBERS: *Serve with soft grainy burger buns.*

LAMB & ROAST VEGGIE ONE-PAN WONDER

There's nothing I love more than a simple, hearty roast for a weekend dinner during the cooler months. But for everyday meals, I skip the heavier cuts and choose lean, flavoursome backstraps, and add plenty of vegetables to get my antioxidant and fibre fix. Packed with garlic and fragrant herbs, this delicious iron-rich dish is one you'll make time and time again, and as a bonus it's so easy to clean up afterwards!

SERVES 4 ♥ PREPARATION TIME: **15 MINS** COOKING TIME: **30 MINS + RESTING**

1 sweet potato,
    cut into wedges
⅓ cup extra virgin olive oil
sea salt
2 lamb backstrap fillets
2 teaspoons tamari
1 cup chopped herbs
    (rosemary and oregano
    leaves work well)
4 garlic cloves, skin on
    and smashed
2 cups green beans, trimmed
2 cups small cauliflower florets
freshly ground black pepper

Preheat the oven to 220°C (200°C fan-forced).

Coat the sweet potato wedges in half the olive oil and place in a roasting tin. Sprinkle with salt and bake for 15 minutes.

Meanwhile, coat the lamb with the tamari and 1 teaspoon olive oil and set aside until the lamb comes to room temperature.

Toss together the herbs and 2 teaspoons olive oil and scatter over the sweet potato. Add the lamb and top with the smashed garlic cloves. Add the beans and cauliflower and drizzle with the remaining oil. Roast for 15 minutes.

Allow the lamb to rest for 5 minutes, then cut it into thin slices. Serve with the roasted vegetables and season generously with salt and pepper.

CHANGE UP THE PROTEIN: *Replace the backstraps with lamb chops, fish, chicken or firm tofu (adjust the cooking times accordingly).*
CHANGE UP THE VEG: *Roasted broccoli and brussels sprouts are fabulous, and both are wonderful for our livers.*
FOR CARB-LOVING FAMILY MEMBERS: *Add kipfler potatoes or more sweet potato.*

Week
Three

Are you trusting yet? Often by week 3, people are feeling clearer in the head and lighter in the body.

At this point, people will often email or call me with comments like:

- I have never eaten so much food and lost so much weight!
- I am finally free of obsession.
- I don't feel like I am being starved.

Once you learn to trust that you can eat, drink and have a normal weight, you really begin to cement this new-found lifestyle. It just becomes your norm.

But don't get so happy that you forget to use the weekends to plan and prep! Our recipes are amazing, but also look at other nutritionist blogs, books and social media. What you are doing is eating low in sugar, low in gluten, high in quality protein, high in satiating fat and a small amount of smart carbs during the day.

Use these recipes as guidelines, but feel free to get adventurous with your own favourite recipes. The other day someone posted their favourite family 'pasta' meal with their Italian grandma's traditional sauce – but instead of white pasta, they served the sauce on browned cauliflower chunks. Yum!

Also, have you found an exercise that is suiting you? If not, please make this part of week three. Make it easy and fun. Remember that HIIT (high-intensity interval training) is a great option for the time-poor person who wants to make friends with their fat storage hormone, insulin.

SIMPLE CURRIED FISH

After a long day at work, my favourite way to unwind is with a meal I can whip up quickly. This dish hits the spot: speedy but full of flavour and brimming with nutrients. Serve it with steamed Asian greens and add a generous squeeze of lime juice for an extra burst of zing. Take it a step further and add a side of cauliflower rice, which is a great source of dietary fibre, omega 3 and lots of B vitamins, and also soaks up all those gorgeous curry flavours.

SERVES 4 ♥ PREPARATION TIME: **15 MINS** COOKING TIME: **15 MINS**

2 teaspoons Thai green
  curry paste
½ cup coconut milk
2 teaspoons coconut sugar
3 teaspoons lime juice
4 x 200 g white fish fillets
  (such as snapper, ling,
  blue-eye trevalla)
⅓ cup shredded coconut
3 teaspoons sesame seeds,
  toasted
¼ cup sesame oil
2 cups chopped Asian greens
  (bok choy, choy sum,
  broccolini)
sea salt
lime wedges, to serve

Preheat the oven to 180°C (160°C fan-forced). Line a baking tray with baking paper.

Combine the curry paste, coconut milk, coconut sugar and lime juice in a small bowl. Coat each piece of fish well in the mixture.

Place the fish on the prepared tray. Sprinkle evenly with the shredded coconut and sesame seeds, then drizzle with half the sesame oil. Bake for 10–15 minutes or until the fish is cooked through.

Meanwhile, steam the Asian greens until just tender. Toss through the remaining sesame oil and season with a pinch of salt.

Divide the fish and greens among plates and serve with lime wedges for squeezing.

FOR CARB-LOVING FAMILY MEMBERS: *Serve with brown rice or noodles.*
CHANGE UP THE PROTEIN: *Replace with GMO-free firm tofu, chickpeas, prawns or chicken tenderloins.*
SPICE IT UP: *Add two chopped red chillies (bird's eye or serrano) to the sesame oil before you drizzle it over the fish.*
NUTRIENT BOOST: *Serve with a side salad, green beans, bean sprouts or snow peas.*

PISTACHIO-CRUSTED PORK

The sweetness of lean protein-packed pork marries so beautifully with the nutty crunch of pistachios. Serve this with a generous side of steamed broccoli; a great liver-cleanser!

SERVES 4 ♥ PREPARATION TIME: **20 MINS** COOKING TIME: **20 MINS+ RESTING**

½ cup raw unsalted shelled
    pistachios, finely crushed
2 teaspoons garlic power
1 teaspoon cayenne pepper
1 teaspoon dried thyme
½ teaspoon ground cinnamon
1 egg
1 x 650 g pork tenderloin,
    trimmed
3 teaspoons olive oil
2 large sweet potatoes,
    peeled and chopped
3 cups broccoli florets
2 teaspoons extra virgin
    olive oil
1 tablespoon finely
    chopped chives
sea salt and freshly
    ground black pepper

Preheat the oven to 200°C (180°C fan-forced).

Combine the pistachios, garlic powder, cayenne, thyme and cinnamon in a small bowl, then spread over a plate. In a separate small bowl, whisk the egg with 1 teaspoon water. Brush the egg wash all over the pork, then press all sides into the pistachio crumb to coat.

Grease a roasting tin with 1 teaspoon olive oil. Add the pork and bake for 15–20 minutes or until cooked through. Transfer the pork to a cutting board and cover loosely with foil, then leave to rest for 10 minutes.

Meanwhile, add the sweet potato and broccoli to a large saucepan of boiling salted water and cook until tender (the broccoli will be done before the sweet potato, so just scoop it out and set aside to drain). Drain the cooked sweet potato well and return to the pan, then add the remaining olive oil and blend with a stick blender until smooth and creamy. Add the chives and season to taste with salt and pepper.

Cut the pork into medallions and serve on a bed of sweet potato mash, with the broccoli alongside.

NUTRIENT BOOST: *Serve with a green salad; something simple like butter lettuce dressed with extra virgin olive oil and lemon juice would go beautifully with this dish.*
CHANGE UP THE PROTEIN: *Replace the pork with chicken thighs or breast fillets; you'll need to adjust the cooking time accordingly.*
GO NUTS: *Use the kind you love the best.*

RAINBOW STIR-FRY

There's a real stigma attached to 'convenience' foods, like pre-packaged spinach leaves and pre-cut salads. I don't share that thinking; I honestly believe that if pre-cut, pre-washed vegetables make you more likely to buy and eat them, then go ahead: just make sure the vegetables are the only ingredient in the bag. We'd all love to have our own organic gardens, ready to pluck a tomato at a moment's notice, but the reality is that we lead busy lives. Here, we use pre-cut coleslaw to whip up a speedy, nutritious stir-fry.

SERVES 4 ♥ PREPARATION TIME: **15 MINS** COOKING TIME: **10 MINS**

2 tablespoons coconut oil
3 brown onions, finely chopped
3 garlic cloves, chopped
1 red chilli (bird's eye or
    serrano), thinly sliced
800 g chicken mince
300 g fresh pre-packaged
    coleslaw mix
500 g mushrooms, sliced
1 zucchini, chopped
2 tablespoons coconut aminos
    (see note)
sea salt and freshly ground
    black pepper
coriander leaves and finely
    sliced spring onion, to serve

Melt the coconut oil in a large wok over high heat. Add the onion, garlic and chilli and cook until softened. Add the chicken mince and stir-fry until it just turns white, breaking it up with a wooden spoon.

Add the coleslaw mix, mushroom and zucchini and stir-fry for 2–3 minutes, then toss through the coconut aminos and season with salt and pepper.

Divide among four bowls and serve hot, garnished with coriander and spring onion.

NOTE: Coconut aminos is a rich, dark sauce made from coconut sap. Salty but also slightly sweet, it's a great substitute for soy sauce or tamari for those avoiding soy and gluten. You can find it at specialty grocers and online.

CHANGE UP THE VEG: *Add any non-starchy vegetables you have in your crisper drawer.*
FOR CARB-LOVING FAMILY MEMBERS: *Add cooked brown rice or chickpeas.*

PANCETTA FRITTATA

If you have a carton of eggs (or just one or two!), you've always got a meal. Eggs are the best protein you can buy and contain the full spectrum of our nutrient-dense amino acids. Packed with protein and good fats, eggs are a nutritional powerhouse — and they're delicious and ultra-versatile, to boot. This is one of my favourite ways to eat eggs; it works for any meal of the day, and any leftovers can be taken to work for lunch.

SERVES 4 ♥ PREPARATION TIME: 15 MINS COOKING TIME: 30 MINS

4 slices pancetta,
   roughly chopped
½ red onion, thinly sliced
8 eggs
2 tablespoons milk
½ teaspoon chopped small
   red chilli
sea salt
½ cup sliced artichoke hearts
½ cup baby rocket,
   plus extra to serve
2 tablespoons basil pesto
¼ cup crumbled goat's or
   cow's feta

Preheat the oven to 200°C (180°C fan-forced).

Heat an ovenproof frying pan over medium heat, add the pancetta and cook for about 3 minutes or until lightly golden. Add the onion and cook for a further 4 minutes or until lightly golden.

Whisk together the eggs, milk, chilli and a pinch of salt and add to the pan, along with the artichoke, rocket and 1 tablespoon pesto. Sprinkle the feta over the top.

Place the pan in the oven, immediately reduce the oven temperature to 180°C (160°C fan-forced) and bake for 20 minutes or until the egg is cooked through. Dollop over the remaining pesto and serve with extra rocket scattered over.

NIX THE PANCETTA: *Go for nitrate-free bacon, grass-fed sausage or smoked salmon instead.*
NUTRIENT BOOST: *Add whatever veggies you've got in your crisper drawer.*
TURN IT INTO BREKKY: *In the morning, I add a slice of buckwheat toast topped with avocado and a drizzle of extra virgin olive oil.*

CHICKEN & CAULIFLOWER BAKE WITH CREAMY TAHINI SAUCE

If your only experience with cauliflower is having it smothered in white sauce and cheese, I urge you to try this cleaner (but still incredibly tasty) version. A fabulous source of vitamins A, C and K, cauliflower is versatile and so, so good for you. I've used chicken thighs here as they are a great source of protein, and their extra fat (compared with chicken breasts) offers more flavour and iron for energy.

SERVES 4 ♥ PREPARATION TIME: **15 MINS** COOKING TIME: **30 MINS**

3 tablespoons extra virgin
   olive oil
1½ tablespoons ground
   coriander (or Moroccan
   spice mix)
8 chicken thigh fillets, sliced
1 head cauliflower,
   broken into florets
4 handfuls of baby rocket
   or baby spinach
1 bunch flat-leaf parsley,
   leaves picked

CREAMY TAHINI SAUCE
½ cup tahini
½ cup lemon juice
⅓ cup water
splash of extra virgin olive oil

Preheat the oven to 220°C (200°C fan-forced). Line a baking tray with baking paper.

Combine the olive oil and ground coriander in a bowl. Remove and reserve half the mixture. Add the chicken to the remaining spiced oil in the bowl and toss to coat well, then set aside to marinate.

Use your hands to coat the cauliflower in the reserved spiced oil. Spread it out on the prepared tray, taking care not to overcrowd it, and roast for 10 minutes. Stir the cauliflower and add the chicken to the tray. Roast for another 20 minutes, stirring halfway through.

Meanwhile, to make the tahini sauce, place all the ingredients in a bowl and mix with a fork or stick blender until smooth and creamy.

Serve the roast chicken and cauliflower on a bed of rocket or spinach, topped with the tahini sauce and parsley.

GO VEGETARIAN: *Use almonds or GMO-free firm tofu for protein, roasting just as you would the chicken, reducing the roasting time accordingly.*
NIX THE TAHINI: *Replace the tahini with a soft goat's cheese or feta, or plain full-fat Greek-style yoghurt.*
FOR CARB-LOVING FAMILY MEMBERS: *Serve with quinoa or brown rice, or add a serve of legumes, such as lentils or chickpeas.*

MOROCCAN SALMON WITH HERBED CAULIFLOWER SALAD

High in essential fatty acids (think beautiful skin), high in protein (think lean muscle mass) and rich in selenium (think fat-burning thyroid control), this simple dish punches well above its weight. Tender salmon pairs so beautifully with the nutty, liver-cleansing cauliflower — if you've never tried it like this, I urge you to give it a go. You may just find it's your new favourite dish!

SERVES 4 ♥ PREPARATION TIME: **20 MINS** COOKING TIME: **10 MINS**

1 teaspoon sweet paprika

1 teaspoon ground cumin

1 teaspoon ground ginger

1 teaspoon freshly ground
   black pepper

½ teaspoon ground cardamom

¼ teaspoon sea salt

1 tablespoon olive oil

4 x 175 g salmon fillets, skin
   and bones removed

**HERBED CAULIFLOWER
   SALAD**

1 teaspoon olive oil

1 cup finely grated cauliflower

2½ cups baby rocket

1 Lebanese cucumber, chopped

½ red onion, chopped

5–6 cherry tomatoes, chopped

3 tablespoons flat-leaf
   parsley leaves

½ cup mint leaves

3 tablespoons lemon juice

¼ teaspoon freshly ground
   black pepper

Combine the paprika, cumin, ginger, pepper, cardamom and salt in a small bowl.

Heat the olive oil in a large frying pan over medium–high heat. Season both sides of the salmon with the spice mixture, then add to the pan and cook for 4–5 minutes each side or until just cooked through (the exact cooking time will depend on the thickness of the fillets). Remove and cover to keep warm.

Meanwhile, to make the cauliflower salad, heat the olive oil in a frying pan over high heat, add the cauliflower and cook, stirring, for 5 minutes or until it becomes crispy. Remove the pan from the heat and add the remaining ingredients. Toss well to combine.

Divide the cauliflower salad among serving plates and top with the salmon.

NUTRIENT BOOST: *Add broccoli to the cauliflower — it tastes great and is high in calcium.*

CHANGE UP THE FISH: *Replace the salmon with any firm white fish fillets (barramundi is particularly good here).*

FOR CARB-LOVING FAMILY MEMBERS: *Add the salad to a bowl of brown rice and mix it up. Kids love a bowl — they think it tastes different, but we know it includes all the same nutrients!*

ANGEL HAIR PASTA WITH CHICKEN & LEMON

It's a rare person who doesn't love sitting down to a comforting bowl of pasta. And while I do enjoy pasta occasionally, I prefer to get my fix with this lighter version; it's still hearty, but without the traditional accompaniments of bloating and sleepiness. This dish offers lots of blood-sugar stabilising protein with a lovely lemon kick. Lemon is fabulous at providing vitamin C, which helps underpin glowing skin.

SERVES 4 ♥ PREPARATION TIME: **15 MINS** COOKING TIME: **20 MINS**

3 x 400 g packets thin
   shirataki or konjac noodles
2 tablespoons extra virgin
   olive oil
800 g chicken breast fillets,
   cut into bite-sized pieces
2 large garlic cloves, crushed
½ teaspoon dried oregano
½ teaspoon sea salt
finely grated zest and juice
   of 1 large lemon
80 g butter
1 tablespoon arrowroot
   (see note)
2 large handfuls baby rocket
2 tablespoons oregano leaves

Prepare the noodles according to the packet instructions, then drain and place in a dry frying pan (without oil) over medium heat. 'Dry roast' them for 1 minute, then set aside.

Heat the olive oil in a large heavy-based frying pan over medium–high heat. Add the chicken, garlic, dried oregano and salt and cook, stirring occasionally, for 8–10 minutes or until the chicken is cooked through. Transfer the chicken mixture to a plate.

Return the pan to medium heat and deglaze with the lemon juice. Add the butter and stir until melted, then whisk in the arrowroot. Add the noodles, chicken mixture and rocket and toss to combine.

Scatter over the lemon zest and oregano leaves and serve.

NOTE: Arrowroot is a gluten-free, paleo-friendly flour. It is low in carbs and we use it here to thicken the sauce. You'll find it in the baking aisle.

SHAKE IT UP: *Add 2 tablespoons of freshly grated parmesan or nutritional yeast (a non-dairy, cheese-flavoured powder that is outrageously tasty).*
GO VEGETARIAN: *Replace the chicken with eggs, GMO-free firm tofu or chickpeas.*
FOR CARB-LOVING FAMILY MEMBERS: *Replace the noodles with spaghetti or rice noodles.*

Week
Four

You got this. Nourishment feeds everything. By now, you are more than likely sleeping better, eating better and hydrating more. You might be feeling lighter, and mentally you're feeling clearer – even kinder.

All of these small steps are leading you to feel better about yourself, and hopefully kindling a desire to go one more step – or three! It is a ripple effect of wellbeing.

Some of the things you now know for sure are that your breakfast can be made in less than 5 minutes, and it will nourish you all morning and stop you dipping into that hangry, brain-fogged space.

Lunch? It's easy! Because you now find yourself automatically making extra dinner each night to turn into a quick, simple and satisfying lunch the next day, perhaps by adding a smart carb to the extra protein, or by adding some protein to the leftover sweet potato or brown rice you cooked for the kids.

If you do ever feel hungry, stop and ask yourself:

- Have I eaten enough protein and fat during my previous meal?
- Did I sleep enough last night?
- Am I thirsty?
- Am I sad or angry at something?

You should not be hungry! You should be nourished. A life of nourishing – how nice is that to make part of your wellbeing?

And so what happens after you complete the 28-day plan in this book? Where do you go? What do you do?

Simply do it again. I hope you will want to continue because you will think: I never felt hungry. I gained energy and confidence, lost my bloat and, well, quite frankly, haven't felt this good since I was in my 20s!

So go on and continue, in your own way, with these principles as the foundation. Create recipes and meal plans that suit your life, or just re-do this entire plan again until it becomes second nature: a new micro habit for life. You can also check in with me on my closed Facebook group (facebook.com/groups/1947572482205029) for more recipes and support.

Successful people are not lucky; they work hard on creating micro habits, slowly – and then they succeed on purpose.

FIESTA BURRITO CUPS

A lot of my clients are surprised to hear that I love Mexican food, and not just as an occasional indulgence. I love meals like burritos and tacos because you can crowd them out with plenty of vegetables, and Mexican spices are fantastic for wellbeing too. This meal, for instance, is high in protein, and by packing in red onion, garlic, tomato, zucchini and spinach, we get a great serve of vegetables and, with them, immune-boosting vitamins A, C and E. Cos lettuce adds iron to our diets, which is necessary for brain health. I love doubling this recipe and taking a serve for lunch the following day.

SERVES **4** ♥ PREPARATION TIME: **15 MINS** COOKING TIME: **35 MINS**

2 tablespoons extra virgin
    olive oil
2 red onions, chopped
2 garlic cloves, chopped
750 g chicken mince
1 tablespoon tomato paste
2 tablespoons Mexican spice
    mix (see page 127 for
    seasoning blends)
2 handfuls baby spinach,
    chopped
2 zucchini, diced
3 tomatoes, diced
2 red capsicums, seeded
    and diced
sea salt and freshly ground
    black pepper
1 large avocado
12 small cos lettuce leaves
1 cup grated cheddar
coriander sprigs, to serve

Heat the olive oil in a large heavy-based frying pan over medium heat. Add the onion and garlic and cook, stirring occasionally, for 5 minutes or until softened.

Working in three batches, add the mince and cook, stirring occasionally, for 5–7 minutes, breaking it up with a wooden spoon. (If you add it all to the pan at once you will not achieve the little bit of browning that adds extra flavour.) Return all the mince to the pan.

Add the tomato paste, Mexican spice mix, spinach, zucchini, tomato and capsicum to the pan and cook, stirring, for another 15 minutes. Season to taste with salt and pepper.

Meanwhile, mash the avocado flesh and season with salt and pepper.

Place three lettuce leaves on each plate, then evenly divide the mince among the leaves. Top with a spoonful of mashed avocado, a sprinkling of cheese and some coriander sprigs. Serve warm.

SPICE IT UP: *Add thinly sliced jalapeno chillies to the mix when browning the protein.*
CHANGE UP THE PROTEIN: *Use grass-fed beef mince, or go for GMO-free firm tofu or prawns.*
FOR CARB-LOVING FAMILY MEMBERS: *Serve on burritos, or with black beans or brown rice.*
MAKE IT DAIRY-FREE: *Replace the cheddar with crumbled goat's cheese or shaved manchego cheese.*

CASHEW & QUINOA STIR-FRY

There's more to protein than steaks and chicken breasts. This recipe uses high-quality vegetarian forms of protein – cashews and quinoa – but believe me, it's the kind of meal you can serve to even the most passionate of meat lovers. Don't skip the coconut milk, or be tempted to use a low-fat version: coconut milk helps strengthen immunity through its antifungal, antibacterial and antiviral properties. It also boosts metabolism, reduces sugar cravings and soothes the digestive system. To protect against cancer, we use turmeric, ginger, onion, bok choy and broccoli; these foods also assist with inflammation. But best of all, this dish is really, really, really tasty. Dig in! A big thanks to Simone on my team at A Healthy View for creating this for hungry vegetarians.

SERVES 4 ♥ PREPARATION TIME: 15 MINS COOKING TIME: 15 MINS

⅔ cup quinoa, rinsed
1 tablespoon coconut oil
2 brown onions, thinly sliced
1 cup finely chopped
   sweet potato
½ teaspoon ground turmeric
2 tablespoons grated ginger
2 cups finely chopped broccoli
sea salt
½ cup coconut milk
3 tablespoons vegetable stock
   or water
1 tablespoon tamari
1 cup raw unsalted cashews
1½ cups roughly chopped
   bok choy
3 tablespoons roughly
   chopped basil leaves
freshly ground black pepper

Cook the quinoa according to the packet instructions (you'll need 2 cups cooked quinoa for the stir-fry).

Meanwhile, heat the coconut oil in a wok over medium heat. Add the onion and cook for 2–3 minutes or until golden.

Add the sweet potato to the wok and stir-fry for 4 minutes or until tender. Stir in the turmeric, ginger, broccoli and ½ teaspoon salt. Add the coconut milk, stock or water, tamari and cashews and stir-fry for 3 minutes. Add the bok choy and basil and season with pepper, then stir-fry for another 3 minutes.

Toss through the quinoa, season to taste with salt and pepper if needed, and serve.

SPICE IT UP: *Chop a bird's eye chilli and add before serving.*
CHANGE UP THE CARBS: *If quinoa's not for you, try brown or basmati rice.*
GO NUTS: *Any kind of nut will work here – use your favourite.*
SWAP THE HERBS: *Try coriander or lemon thyme in place of basil.*

SPEEDY MISO FISH

Many people think that fish is too complicated to cook at home, but it really isn't. In this recipe, dulse and nori flakes bring with them a quick, easy umami flavour. Traditionally added to rice dishes in Japan, they lend a rich savoury note and are a great source of vitamins A and C. Find them in Asian supermarkets and selected grocery stores.

SERVES 4 ♥ PREPARATION TIME: **15 MINS** COOKING TIME: **15 MINS**

4 bunches broccolini, trimmed

1 tablespoon extra virgin olive oil

4 x 175 g white fish fillets (such as ling, blue-eye trevalla or coral trout), skin and bones removed

sea salt and freshly ground black pepper

⅓ cup whole-egg mayonnaise

¼ cup white miso paste

2 tablespoons rice wine vinegar

2 teaspoons dulse or nori flakes and/or sesame seeds

Preheat the oven to 200°C (180°C fan-forced).

Place the broccolini on a baking tray and drizzle with half the olive oil. Bake for 5 minutes.

Coat the fish fillets with the remaining olive oil, season with salt and pepper and place on top of the broccolini. Bake for 10 minutes or until the broccolini is tender and the fish is cooked through.

Meanwhile, combine the mayonnaise, miso and vinegar in a bowl.

Drizzle the miso dressing over the fish and serve with the broccolini. Finish with a sprinkling of flakes and/or sesame seeds.

CHANGE UP THE VEG: *Replace the broccolini with green beans, snow peas or half a head cauliflower, chopped into bite-sized pieces.*

CHANGE UP THE DRESSING: *If miso's not your thing, try making sesame mayo instead by stirring 1–2 teaspoons sesame oil into the mayonnaise.*

GO VEGETARIAN: *Replace the fish with GMO-free firm tofu.*

SPICED CHICKEN SKEWERS

Sometimes a little planning goes a long way. Prepping this recipe the night before to allow for a long marinating time helps create a tasty, healthy meal the following evening. This is the kind of dish that would be great at a weekend barbecue, but it's equally fab on a weeknight. You could use a packaged spice mix to save time if you like.

You'll need eight wooden skewers for the chicken. Soak them for at least 20 minutes (or up to 3 hours) so they won't burn during cooking.

SERVES 4 ♥ PREPARATION TIME: **20 MINS + MARINATING** COOKING TIME: **15 MINS**

2 tablespoons extra virgin
   olive oil
2 small red onions, chopped
2 tablespoons curry powder
2 teaspoons ground turmeric
½ teaspoon ground cumin
½ teaspoon ground coriander
½ teaspoon ground cinnamon
2 garlic cloves,
   roughly chopped
½ cup coconut milk
3 jalapeno chillies, seeded
   and roughly chopped
3 tablespoons chopped
   coriander leaves
3 cm piece of ginger,
   roughly chopped
juice of 1 lemon, plus extra
   wedges to serve
¼ teaspoon sea salt
4 chicken breast fillets (about
   700 g), cut into 2 cm pieces
3 capsicums (red, yellow or
   orange), seeded and cut
   into 2 cm pieces
2 zucchini, cut into 2 cm pieces
green salad, to serve

Heat 2 teaspoons of the olive oil in a small frying pan over medium heat. Add the onion, curry powder and ground spices and cook, stirring often, for 5 minutes or until fragrant and the onion has softened.

Transfer the onion mixture to a blender, add the garlic, coconut milk, jalapeno, coriander leaves, ginger, lemon juice and salt, and blend until smooth. Transfer to a large shallow dish. Add the chicken and turn to coat well, then cover and marinate in the fridge for 24 hours.

Thread the capsicum, zucchini and chicken alternately onto the soaked skewers. Brush a frying pan or chargrill pan with the remaining oil and heat over medium heat. Add the skewers and cook for 5–7 minutes each side or until the chicken is cooked through. You could also cook the skewers on the barbecue if you like.

The skewers are perfect served with lemon wedges and a big green salad.

FOR CARB-LOVING FAMILY MEMBERS: *Add a side of rice or orzo pasta tossed with basil pesto.*
NUTRIENT BOOST: *Add a side of roasted or barbecued broccoli, dressed with extra virgin olive oil and lemon, or basil pesto.*
ADD SOME SASSY SPICING: *Include some garam masala. This is often used in Indian cooking to add spice in a mild way.*
UP THE PROTEIN: *Sprinkle your choice of seeds (sesame, pumpkin, flax etc) over the salad.*

SPICED FISH WITH ZUCCHINI NOODLES

Fish is the ultimate fast food, and much better for your body and mind than anything from a drive-thru! This recipe is testament to that fact — packed with Cajun spices and ready in minutes, it's the kind of weeknight dinner you'll be racing home for.

SERVES 4 ♥ PREPARATION TIME: **10 MINS** COOKING TIME: **15 MINS**

4 x 175 g white fish fillets
(such as snapper, john dory
or barramundi), skin and
bones removed
⅓ cup Cajun spice mix
¼ cup extra virgin olive oil
4 garlic cloves, crushed
4 zucchini, spiralised
500 g cherry tomatoes
sea salt and freshly ground
black pepper
lemon wedges and flat-leaf
parsley leaves, to serve

Coat the fish fillets in the Cajun spice mix and set aside.

Heat 1 tablespoon olive oil in each of two large frying pans over medium heat. Add the fish fillets to one of the pans and cook for 3–5 minutes each side or until the fish is golden and a little crispy.

Meanwhile, add the crushed garlic to the other pan and cook for 2 minutes, stirring occasionally, or until it just starts to brown. Add the zucchini, tomatoes and remaining olive oil to the pan, stir to combine and season to taste with salt and pepper. Cook for 3–5 minutes to heat through.

Divide the zucchini noodles and tomatoes among plates and place the fish on top. Serve with lemon wedges and plenty of flat-leaf parsley.

FOR CARB-LOVING FAMILY MEMBERS: *Add a side of roasted sweet potato, or serve on a bed of pasta or soba noodles.*
HERB ADDICTION: *Add torn basil or lemon thyme to the zucchini during cooking.*

STICKY CHINESE-STYLE PORK

As a nutritionist, I hear a lot of myths about food. One thing I hear time and again is that pork is 'bad' for you. Sure, eating bacon for every meal, every day isn't going to set you on the path to great health, but lean pork is actually an incredible protein option. Rich in thiamin, niacin, B6 and B12, selenium, zinc and omega 3, pork is a lean muscle maker of epic proportions. It works so beautifully with Asian flavours too, which we've used here to very good effect — there is something so gorgeous about the marriage of sweet, salty and nutty flavours.

SERVES 4 ♥ PREPARATION TIME: **15 MINS + MARINATING** COOKING TIME: **30 MINS & RESTING**

2 tablespoons tamari
1 tablespoon Chinese five-spice
1 garlic clove, finely chopped
2 tablespoons raw honey
2 tablespoons sesame oil
2 tablespoons lime juice
1 x 650 g pork fillet
2 teaspoons chilli oil
2 cups chopped broccolini
2 cups chopped choy sum
chopped red chilli (bird's eye
    or serrano), to serve
finely sliced spring onion,
    to serve

Combine the tamari, Chinese five-spice, garlic, honey, sesame oil and lime juice in a glass bowl.

Add the pork and turn to coat in the marinade. Set aside in the fridge for at least 30 minutes and up to 2 hours if you have time.

Preheat the oven to 200°C (180°C fan-forced).

Pour 1 cm water into the base of a roasting tin, then position a wire rack over the water. Drain the pork and set the marinade aside. Place the pork on the rack and roast for 20–25 minutes or until cooked, turning halfway through and basting with the reserved marinade every few minutes. Remove from the oven and rest for 10 minutes.

While the pork is resting, heat a wok over high heat and add the chilli oil. Once hot, add the broccolini and stir-fry for 2 minutes. Add the choy sum and stir-fry for a further 2 minutes until tender and crispy.

Slice the pork and serve with the stir-fried greens alongside. Garnish with chopped chilli and spring onion.

FOR CARB-LOVING FAMILY MEMBERS: *Serve with basmati rice and cooked peas.*
CHANGE UP THE PROTEIN: *Replace the pork with chicken or white fish fillets, adjusting the cooking times accordingly.*

ZESTY LENTIL SOUP

Lentils may be small but, boy, are they powerful. They are low-carb and a tasty source of protein and cholesterol-lowering fibre. They help with blood-sugar disorders because their high-fibre component prevents blood sugar rising rapidly after a meal, and they're packed with vitamin B as well. These tiny nutritional nuggets fill you up, but not out! Here I use red lentils but if you are short of time you could use split red lentils; just halve the cooking time. Like all soups, this one tastes better after settling for a day or two, so make it ahead if you can.

SERVES 4–6 ♥ PREPARATION TIME: **20 MINS** COOKING TIME: **30 MINS**

1 tablespoon extra virgin
   olive oil
2 brown onions, chopped
2 cups chopped baby carrots
6 garlic cloves, chopped
2 teaspoons ground cumin
2 teaspoons ground coriander
2 teaspoons ground turmeric
1 teaspoon ground cinnamon
1 teaspoon freshly ground
   black pepper
2 teaspoons harissa paste
1.5 litres vegetable or
   chicken stock
2 cups water
1 small head cauliflower, broken
   into bite-sized florets
1½ cups red lentils, rinsed well
1 x 400 g tin diced tomatoes,
   with no added salt
2 tablespoons tomato paste
200 g baby spinach
⅓ cup lemon juice
½ cup coriander leaves
finely grated zest of 1 lemon

Heat the olive oil in a large heavy-based saucepan or flameproof casserole dish over medium heat. Add the onion and carrot and cook, stirring occasionally, for 6–8 minutes or until softened. Toss in the garlic and cook for 2 minutes.

Add the ground spices and harissa paste and stir for 1 minute to warm through. Pour in the stock and water, then add the cauliflower, lentils, tinned tomatoes and tomato paste. Bring to the boil, then reduce the heat and simmer, stirring occasionally, for 15 minutes or until the lentils are tender but not mushy.

Just before serving, stir in the spinach and lemon juice. Ladle into bowls and finish with the coriander leaves and a sprinkling of lemon zest.

UP THE FIBRE: *Sprinkle whole flaxseeds into the soup before serving.*
FOR CARB-LOVING FAMILY MEMBERS: *Serve with grainy, crunchy bread.*
FOR CHEESE LOVERS: *Scatter over some finely grated parmesan just before serving, or crumble over some goat's cheese or manchego.*

References

CHAPTER 1: WHAT DOES YOUR WORLD LOOK LIKE?

Page 22 Eat an adequate amount of protein throughout the course of the day and you might just sleep easier ...: H. Fukushige et al., 'Effects of tryptophan-rich breakfast and light exposure during the daytime on melatonin secretion at night', *Journal of Physiological Anthropology*, 2014, Nov 19; 33: 33. doi: 10.1016/j.ecl.2013.05.001

Page 22 Lack of sleep can affect not only our sleep hormones, but also our fat storage hormone, insulin ...: Omar Mesarwi et al., 'Sleep disorders and the development of insulin resistance and obesity', *Endocrinology and Metabolism Clinics of North America*, 2013, vol. 42, no. 3, pp. 617–34. doi: 10.1016/j. ecl.2013.05.001

Page 27 63% of Australian adults are overweight or obese, along with one in four children and adolescents...: Australian Institute of Health and Welfare, *Australia's Health 2018*, 20 June 2018, aihw.gov.au/ reports/australias-health/australias-health-2018/contents/indicators-of-australias-health/proportion-of-people-obese-and-overweight

Page 27 Being overweight or obese also increases our risk of several cancers...: Cancer Council, 'Overweight, obesity and cancer', n.d., cancercouncil.com.au/1in3cacers/ lifestyle-choices-and-cancer/overweight-obesity-and-cancer/#rerXux8YfozSD8SB.99

Page 27 Are you surprised to hear that being depressed is a risk factor for being overweight? ...: Elizabeth Goodman & Robert C. Whitaker, 'A prospective study of the role of depression in the development and persistence of adolescent obesity', *Pediatrics*, 2002, vol. 110, no. 3, pp. 497–504

Page 27 One in five Australians aged 16–85 years will experience a mental illness in any year...: Beyond Blue, 'Who does it affect?', n.d., beyondblue.org.au/who-does-it-affect

Page 27 The SMILES trial ...: Food & Mood Centre, Deakin University, n.d., foodandmoodcentre.com.au/media/ smiles-trial/

CHAPTER 2: THE ABSOLUTE, ULTIMATE, BEST DIET EVER

Page 37 Dr Stephen Sinatra, one of the wisest integrative cardiologists of our time...: Dr Stephen Sinatra, 'The Great Cholesterol Myth', n.d., drsinatra.com/the-great-cholesterol-myth

Page 47 As we saw earlier, studies are increasingly showing the important role good nutrition plays in our mental wellbeing...: Food & Mood Centre, Deakin University, n.d., foodandmoodcentre.com.au/media/ smiles-trial/

Page 60 New research suggests that drinking artificially sweetened drinks is associated with diabetes...: Brian Hoffmann et al., 'The Influence of Sugar and Artificial Sweeteners on Vascular Health during the Onset and Progression of Diabetes', *The FASEB Journal*, April 2018, fasebj.org/doi/abs/10.1096/fasebj.2018.32.1_supplement.603.20

CHAPTER 3: HOW TO GET IT RIGHT IN YOUR WORLD

Page 76 A recent study with over 200 participants undergoing a sleep-restricted week...: Guglielmo Beccuti & Silvana Pannain, 'Sleep and obesity', *Current Opinion in Clinical Nutrition and Metabolic Care*, 2011, vol. 14, no. 4, pp. 402–12. doi: 10.1097/MCO.0b013e3283479109

Page 79 In a study of over 2000 participants ...: Michael A. Grandner et al., 'The Relationship between Sleep Duration and Body Mass Index Depends on Age', *Obesity* (Silver Spring), 2015, vol. 23, no. 12, pp. 2491–8. doi: 10.1002/oby.21247

Page 82 Some studies show that just 20 minutes of this type of exercise each day can be effective for weight loss...: Damon L. Swift et al., 'The Role of Exercise and Physical Activity in Weight Loss and Maintenance', *Progress in Cardiovascular Diseases*, 2014, vol. 56, no. 4, pp. 441–7. doi: 10.1016/j.pcad.2013.09.012

CHAPTER 4: PREPARING FOR THE PLAN

Page 130 These results provide further evidence that coffee drinking ...: Erikka Loftfield et al., 'Association of Coffee Drinking With Mortality by Genetic Variation in Caffeine Metabolism: Findings From the UK Biobank', *JAMA Internal Medicine*, 2018, vol. 178, no. 8, pp 1086–97/doi: 10.1001/jamainternmed.2018.2425

Sneaky names for hidden sugars

Agave nectar

Brown rice solids

Cane juice, crystals or syrup

Concentrates such as fruit juice, grape juice

Corn sweetener or syrup solids

Dextran

Dextrose

Diastase or diastase malt

Fructose (any form)

Fruit juice or concentrate

Glucose (any form)

Honey

Lactose

Malts such as barley, diastase

Maltodextrin

Maltose

Molasses

Sucanat

Sucrose

Sugars such as beet, brown, cane, corn, date, golden, grape, icing, turbinado

Syrups such as agave, buttered, cane carob, high-fructose corn, golden, grape, invert, maple, refiners', sorghum, treacle

Acknowledgements

The team at Pan Macmillan

Ingrid Ohlsson, you are one inspiring publisher. When I came to you to pitch this book, you didn't blink, you said yes immediately. It is an honour to have your trust and belief in my work and passion for nutrition. And birds of a feather flock together, your team has been nothing short of exceptional. Virginia Birch, thank you for your endless insight into how to create a flow that a reader will enjoy, and for your eagle eyes. You have been my wings and I am eternally grateful. Naomi van Groll, thank you for keeping me in check and keeping us on task in the kitchen and at the computer.

To the three outstanding women who made this book a visual feast with photography, styling and cooking – Cath Muscat, Vanessa Austin and Sarah Mayoh – you are a trifecta of gorgeousness. Thanks also to designer Arielle Gamble for her clever, colourful design and beautiful illustrations.

Wellness Leaders

Thank you to my deep-thinking colleagues in my corporate world, schools or organisations who value wellbeing. You get me, because, like me, you truly know that wellness – through good nutrition intertwined with sleep, exercise and connection – underpins everything: personal growth, business productivity, mental resilience, immune system and even a kind heart. Peter Joseph from the Black Dog Institute, Robert Easton from Accenture, Darren Steinberg from Dexus, Chelsea Pottenger from EQ Consulting, Ruben Young from AMP, Nikki Kinloch from CureCancer, Jamie Oliver, Emma Isaacs from Business Chicks and Sir Anthony Seldon from The University of Buckingham.

My Tribe

Steven, Gabi, Jake, Holly Dolly & Hampy – I love you more than a million avocados.

Conversion Chart

Measuring cups and spoons may vary slightly from one country to another, but the difference is generally not enough to affect a recipe. All cup and spoon measures are level.

One Australian metric measuring cup holds 250 ml (8 fl oz), one Australian tablespoon holds 20 ml (4 teaspoons) and one Australian metric teaspoon holds 5 ml. North America, New Zealand and the UK use a 15 ml (3-teaspoon) tablespoon.

LENGTH

METRIC	IMPERIAL
3 mm	⅛ inch
6 mm	¼ inch
1 cm	½ inch
2.5 cm	1 inch
5 cm	2 inches
18 cm	7 inches
20 cm	8 inches
23 cm	9 inches
25 cm	10 inches
30 cm	12 inches

LIQUID MEASURES

ONE AMERICAN PINT	ONE IMPERIAL PINT
500 ml (16 fl oz)	600 ml (20 fl oz)

CUP	METRIC	IMPERIAL
⅛ cup	30 ml	1 fl oz
¼ cup	60 ml	2 fl oz
⅓ cup	80 ml	2½ fl oz
½ cup	125 ml	4 fl oz
⅔ cup	160 ml	5 fl oz
¾ cup	180 ml	6 fl oz
1 cup	250 ml	8 fl oz
2 cups	500 ml	16 fl oz
2¼ cups	560 ml	20 fl oz
4 cups	1 litre	32 fl oz

DRY MEASURES

The most accurate way to measure dry ingredients is to weigh them. However, if using a cup, add the ingredient loosely to the cup and level with a knife; don't compact the ingredient unless the recipe requests 'firmly packed'.

METRIC	IMPERIAL
15 g	½ oz
30 g	1 oz
60 g	2 oz
125 g	4 oz (¼ lb)
185 g	6 oz
250 g	8 oz (½ lb)
375 g	12 oz (¾ lb)
500 g	16 oz (1 lb)
1 kg	32 oz (2 lb)

OVEN TEMPERATURES

CELSIUS	FAHRENHEIT
100°C	200°F
120°C	250°F
150°C	300°F
160°C	325°F
180°C	350°F
200°C	400°F
220°C	425°F

CELSIUS	GAS MARK
110°C	¼
130°C	½
140°C	1
150°C	2
170°C	3
180°C	4
190°C	5
200°C	6
220°C	7
230°C	8
240°C	9
250°C	10

Index

First published 2019 in Macmillan
by Pan Macmillan Australia Pty Limited
Level 25, 1 Market Street, Sydney, New South Wales
Australia 2000

A CIP catalogue record for this book is available
from the National Library of Australia: http://
catalogue.nla.gov.au

Design by Arielle Gamble
Edited by Katri Hilden and Rachel Carter
Prop and food styling by Vanessa Austin
Food preparation by Sarah Mayoh
Colour + reproduction by Splitting Image
Colour Studio
Printed in China by 1010 Printing International Ltd

10 9 8 7 6 5 4 3 2 1